WHERE FREEDOM GREW

Freedom has always been a basic principle of American democracy. The desire for the freedom to choose their own way of life led the Colonists to the break with England, to the Revolutionary War, to independence.

Many of the places where the ideas of liberty and freedom grew to importance still exist today. Here you can see them, in exquisite photographs that bring an immediacy to the ideals that brought our country into being.

As the text follows the course of the Revolutionary War, you see Boston's Old South Meeting House, Faneuil Hall, Paul Revere's home, Old North Church, Buckman's tavern where the Minutemen assembled, Concord bridge, the church where Patrick Henry asked for liberty or death, Independence Hall, the conference house on Staten Island, and more. Many are familiar; some are lesser known but significant in the fight for freedom; all are shown in stunning photographic detail.

WHERE FREEDOM GREW is a handsome book that will stir the hearts of all Americans, young or old. A list of current addresses indicating where to find these landmarks is included.

Where
Freedom
Grew

by Bob Stubenrauch

Photographs by the author

Dodd, Mead & Company

New York

917.3

For my sons, David and Bruce

FRONTISPIECE: *The Concord River at Concord, Massachusetts*

Acknowledgments

I wish to thank the following organizations for their generous cooperation:
   The Philadelphia Maritime Museum
   The Valley Forge Park Commission
   Independence National Historical Park, Pennsylvania
   The Carpenters' Company, Philadelphia
   The Elfreth's Alley Association, Philadelphia
   Christ Church of Philadelphia
   The John Bartram Association, Philadelphia
   The Fairmont Park Commission, Philadelphia
   Washington Crossing State Park Commission, Pennsylvania
   Washington Crossing State Park, New Jersey
   McKonkey Ferry Museum, New Jersey
   Morristown National Historical Park, New Jersey
   St. John's Episcopal Church, Richmond, Virginia
   Colonial Williamsburg Inc., Williamsburg, Virginia
   Yorktown Battlefield, Colonial National Historical Park, Virginia
   The Berkeley Plantation, Virginia
   The Delaware State Museum, Dover, Delaware
   Raynham Hall Advisory Committee, Town of Oyster Bay, Long Island, New
      York
   Paul Revere Memorial Association, Boston
   Lexington Historical Society, Lexington, Massachusetts
   The Lexington Minute Men, Inc., Lexington, Massachusetts
   Corporation of Christ Church, Boston
   Old South Association, Boston
   The Conference House Association, Inc., Staten Island, New York
   The Congregation Jeshuat Israel, Touro Synagogue, Newport, Rhode Island
   Nassau County Division of Parks, New York

Photographs of the John Dickinson home were taken through the courtesy of
the Delaware State Archives and Leon deValinger, Jr., State Archivist. I would
also like to thank the following individuals: Charles Frost, Harold Atkinson, Emma
Cocker, Mrs. E. L. Martin, Mrs. James F. Neugent, Elizabeth Howe, George F.
Gabriel, Wendy R. Davis, Fred Hansen, and Rabbi Lewis of Touro Synagogue.

   A special word of thanks is due my wife, without whose help and encourage-
ment this book could not have been done.

"We hold these truths to be self-evident, that all men are created equal, that they are endowed by their Creator with certain unalienable Rights, that among these are Life, Liberty and the pursuit of Happiness."

Declaration of Independence
1776

Contents

Preface

The causes of the American Revolution went back decades before the shots fired on Lexington Green. The attitudes of the King and the British Parliament were inflexible: the colonies were possessions and the inhabitants were subjects. The judgment of the Crown was not to be questioned. Should the Royal Navy need seamen, impress them in America. If the treasury was impoverished by foreign wars, tax the Americans.

To the colonists who carved farms out of America's wilderness, who fished the seas in ships they built from her towering forests, America was a country, a part of England. As free Englishmen, the colonists expected to enjoy the basic rights of the Magna Carta. Accustomed to local self-government in their town meetings and houses of representatives, they resented arbitrary edicts from a remote monarchy. Had the ministry and Parliament been more understanding and more just, America might have become a dominion of the British Empire. More than distance separated the Old World and the New, however, and independence was probably inevitable.

What was this New World like? Was it the world seen in the romantic paintings of the period—formal pictures of formal men, anonymous men in powdered wigs? Were the battles of the American Revolution crisp, color-splashed expanses of orderly ranks advancing across verdant landscapes to meet neat rows of well-groomed enemies?

There were a few battles astonishing in their color, pomp, and grandeur, but they were the exception. This was not a war of simple challenges and prompt victories. It was a war of many sides involving persons from many walks of life. The British army was confident, experienced, invincible. For the ugly, hard work ahead, there were hired mercenaries, the Hessians, equally skilled and proud. Against them, brave and hesitant both, wise in the ways of the bay and the forest but ignorant of tactics, strategy and discipline, were the colonials. Farmers, artisans, seamen, merchants, the humble who could not write, and the aristocracy learned in Latin and Greek drew together for a common purpose.

Their world was a silver-gray world—the color of weathered split-rail fences, homespun clothes, and the dented pewter plates on the table. It was a quiet world, largely—the ring of the axe in the wood lot, the distant church bell, the hum of nature in the fields. It was a world where life was uncertain; a man could live to be eighty, or bury his six children in two weeks of the dreaded summer fever, typhoid.

The colonists drew together and finally fought together fitfully for eight years. Not all of them, though. The greatest army was the one that never marched, never left home. Though they wanted peace and freedom, these were the uncommitted. They sat on the sidelines to see if a handful could work a miracle, and when it was over many must have wondered what they would tell their children. The Loyalists had their convictions too, and formed their regiments with the Crown, though never as many as Britain expected.

The patriots did not fully know what they wanted in victory. In peace they almost agreed to settle for nothing—thirteen independent states, each alone, free but weak. Only the vision of a group of men of astonishing brilliance and virtuosity insisted on forging a strong central government and a flexible Constitution, to grow and change in a future none could dream of. All the ancient wrongs of kings and despots were forever denied in a Bill of Rights, to protect individual liberties. No system of self-government has worked as well as America's democracy. The dedication of each new generation to resolve to make it work is vital. The system is only as good as the people make it.

Here are some of the houses, the churches, the rooms, the fields, and rivers these colonial patriots knew. These are the floors they walked, the fireplaces they warmed themselves before. Here are the chairs and tables, the drafty huts, the slopes where their bones lie. Here is where some few of them lived and worked, fought and hoped.

This is where freedom grew.

WHERE
FREEDOM
GREW

Elfreth's Alley, basically unchanged in two hundred years.

Built by Thomas Potts between 1724 and 1728, houses No. 120 and 122 are the oldest surviving buildings in the Alley. Ben Franklin met with friends at No. 122 for many years.

1735

Elfreth's Alley

Philadelphia, Pennsylvania

IT IS understandable that the imposing brick mansions of the colonial aristocracy should endure into our time. They were built to last and were frequently occupied by descendants of the same family for a century or more. It is unusual to find well-preserved homes of ordinary workers or artisans of the eighteenth century remaining in the heart of a modern city. Elfreth's Alley is an entire street of such modest homes, recalling a lesser economic level of colonial life.

In 1714, the alley was laid out to provide easier access to a mill and a blacksmith shop. By the end of the century, scores of people of every skill and calling had occupied homes here. Some lived in Elfreth's Alley only a year or two, others for a lifetime. Adam Clampffer was a hatter, William Will a pewterer. William Atkinson was a Quaker shipwright, John Ackley, a Windsor chairmaker and Bowyer Brooke was a boatbuilder. There was a locksmith, a nailsmith, a privateer captain, a tailor, sailors, and bakers. It was logical that a man with interests in every field would find friends here, and Benjamin Franklin did. His "junta," or club, met regularly in the rooms of William Maugridge, a carpenter, the tenant of No. 122.

Many of the people who lived in Elfreth's Alley had links with Revolutionary leaders. Cabinetmaker William Wayne was a cousin of General Anthony Wayne. A potter's daughter, Hannah Meyer, married the Reverend John Muhlenberg, the "fighting parson" of the Revolution. Captain William

Where Freedom Grew

Clymer was a builder in the alley; his nephew was George Clymer, a signer of the Declaration of Independence.

Elfreth's Alley was touched with the same hardships of colonial life that existed anywhere in America. A sailor left on a privateer and never returned, a sawyer drowned in the Delaware, a smithy had his forges seized by the British. One woman was widowed four times; one man similarly had five wives. A Quaker was disowned for doing military service, another Tory Quaker was hung for serving as gatekeeper for the British during the occupation of 1778.

Cophey Doughlas lived here with his wife Phoebe and their children for ten years. Across the street from this Negro family lived Moses Mordecai, an early member of Mikveh Israel congregation. In these thirty-odd houses the practical harmony of democracy has been practiced for over 250 years.

A second-floor bedroom. Most of the houses were three-story brick structures with one main room on each floor connected by narrow staircases. Unusual features were built-in closets (instead of cabinets) and high mantels over tiny fireplaces.

1740

The John Bartram House

Philadelphia, Pennsylvania

IN THE years before the Revolution most of the colonists were isolated from the knowledge and sciences of Europe. Thrown on their own resources, many sought careers without benefit of formal training. One of these was a brilliant Quaker, John Bartram, of Darby, Pennsylvania. At the age of twenty-nine he bought a hundred-acre farm on the swift Schuylkill River and built a rambling stone house with his own hands.

John Bartram built his house of local gneiss stone in 1731, decorating the stone window frames with carvings.

A second-floor room with many cupboards.

A reluctant farmer, he turned more and more to his consuming interest: the study of seeds and plants, trees, and everything in nature. A keen and accurate observer, he wandered farther and farther on each field trip, from Florida to Lake Ontario, returning home after long months with his saddlebags heavy with seed and his journals crammed with meticulous notes.

His early interest in medicine led to a local reputation as a self-taught physician. In the years before the Revolution his friends included Dr. Benjamin Rush, later the surgeon general of the Continental armies, Benjamin Franklin, and the Pennsylvania statesman, James Logan. Bartram's skills and knowledge as the leading botanist in the colonies were recognized in England by a fellow Quaker and amateur plant collector, Peter Collinson. A remarkable correspondence of almost forty years duration ensued and led to Bartram sending

An unusual split-step staircase leads to rooms on the second floor.

thousands of specimens to Europe. In 1765, King George III appointed him Royal Botanist to the Crown at a salary of fifty pounds a year.

Bartram managed his farm and gardens despite his travels, freed his slaves and retained them as paid servants, raised eleven children, and lived into the second year of the war, 1777. His advancement of scientific knowledge although lacking a formal education, was a reflection of the atmosphere in the colonies at the time. Free of Europe's caste system and traditions, Americans were daring to do what their talents and energy allowed, already thinking of themselves as independent people.

In a small room to the right of the main entrance is this stove, a gift to John Bartram from its designer, Benjamin Franklin.

This second-floor room was an infant's bed chamber. The third floor was divided into a warren of tiny rooms for Bartram's many children.

A devout Quaker, John Bartram was ejected from the Society of Friends for some imagined conflict between his faith and his scientific interests. When he made house alterations in 1770, he carved his credo in bold letters and set it in the wall. It reads: IT IS GOD ALONE ALMYTY LORD, THE HOLY ONE BY ME ADOR'D, JOHN BARTRAM 1770.

A huge stone barn adjoins a smaller structure which Bartram called his seed house.

A pantry near the front entrance. Windows were propped open with a stick.

Planted in Bartram's lifetime, this yellow-wood tree (Cladrastis lutea) is a native of the southern states.

Christ Church in Philadelphia is an architectural landmark, as it was in Revolutionary days. Its chancel is marked by the first Palladian window in America. The "wineglass" pulpit was a popular design of the times. The branched chandelier has hung over the center aisle for 225 years.

1754

Christ Church

Philadelphia, Pennsylvania

FOUNDED in 1695, Christ Church in Philadelphia has been called "The Nation's Church." Few churches have had as many leaders of the nation worship within their walls. Its list of founders included carpenters, judges, physicians, merchants, a dyer, and a baker. Two of the gentlemen gave their occupations simply as "pirate." Their forays into the Red Sea must have been successful, since each donated one thousand pounds.

After many changes and enlargements, the present Georgian-style structure was completed in 1744. Its 200-foot tower and steeple took another ten years and became a mariners' landmark.

The rector of Christ Church in colonial days was Bishop William White. He was devoted to the cause of liberty and the sermons preached in his church during 1775 by the Reverends Smith and Duche caused considerable controversy in Europe. Offering advice on "spiritual and temporal liberties" and

The pews and tile floor date from post-colonial restoration. Locations of pews of colonial notables are marked for visitors.

the perils of "arbitrary and alien rule" was considered inappropriate from a Church of England pulpit. Yet hardly a leading patriot from Washington to Adams failed to read these widely distributed sermons. When the Declaration of Independence was signed, Bishop White opened the service book of the liturgy and struck out the prayers for the King as no longer appropriate.

Seven signers of the Declaration are buried within and without the walls of Christ Church, notably Benjamin Franklin, Robert Morris, Dr. Benjamin Rush, and Francis Hopkinson.

Christ Church has always been associated with the birth of the nation. In 1777, a bolt of lightning dramatized the sermons that had been delivered in the church by striking and destroying the Royal Crown of England atop the lofty steeple.

Architectural style is colonial in the Georgian spirit. Dr. John Kearsley, who later worked on Independence Hall, is credited with the design. Graves are both outside and inside the walls.

The 200-foot spire that took ten years to build. Benjamin Franklin headed one of several fund-raising lotteries for its construction.

1762

The George Wythe House

Williamsburg, Virginia

BORN in Virginia in 1726, George Wythe lived through a crucial period of colonial history and strongly influenced its course. He completed his studies at William and Mary College and was admitted to the bar in 1747. In 1755, he moved into the stately brick house on Williamsburg's Palace Street with his bride, Elizabeth. Her father, Richard Taliaferro, was an amateur architect of some note, and the home he presented them was to be the meeting place of dozens of famous Americans.

While a member of the House of Burgesses, Wythe tutored a promising student of nineteen, named Thomas Jefferson, in his home. In 1765, he drafted a remonstrance against the Stamp Act and indicated a growing concern over Britain's contempt for colonial rights. Wythe was a delegate to the Continental Congress in 1775 and was the first of the Virginia party to sign the Declaration of Independence.

George Wythe was mayor of Williamsburg and for eleven years was professor of law at William and Mary. Henry Clay and John Marshall were among his students. He was a great influence in the difficult task of attaining ratification for the new nation's Constitution in 1787, and molded a generation of leaders in his concept of freedom under law.

His grave is in a quiet Virginia churchyard, a short distance from the church where he heard Patrick Henry declare for "liberty or death."

*Formal gardens surround a bowling green behind the main house. The struc-
ture at left is the poultry house.*

*Huge paired chimneys provide fireplaces in all eight rooms. Windows of the
second floor have smaller panes, creating an illusion of added height.*

The dining room is furnished with English and American pieces of the period, typical of the well-to-do eighteenth-century Virginian.

The parlor is distinguished by a beautiful fireplace.

This housewife's bedroom has been furnished to reflect typical occupations of her day: crewel work, embroidery, and use of the tape loom.

George Wythe tutored promising students in his home, having no children of his own. This scientific apparatus, including a model of the solar system, is typical of that used in his day.

The gardens were surrounded by several buildings, similar to plantation arrangements but on a smaller scale. These included a kitchen, a smokehouse, a laundry, and a lumber house.

1767

Old South Meeting-House

Boston, Massachusetts

*I*N COLONIAL America, the town church was usually the largest structure erected, serving a dual purpose as a place of worship and a meeting house. Old South Church has such a double history. It saw the development of religious practice from the strict and narrow Puritan beliefs to a more liberal faith. As a political meeting house, it was the scene of bitter sessions that occurred with growing frequency until the British finally evacuated Boston in 1776.

In 1729, the old cedar church in which Benjamin Franklin had been baptized, dating from 1669, was torn down. The brick building that was to see so much history was dedicated in 1730.

In 1768, an angry town meeting overflowed Faneuil Hall and moved to Old South. On this occasion James Otis led a delegation to compel Governor Francis Bernard to remove from the harbor a British warship stationed there to enforce the odious impressment and customs laws.

In March of 1770, emotions were at fever pitch over the Boston Massacre. Old South was jammed with thousands of patriots late into the night until Samuel Adams was able to announce that Lieutenant-Governor Thomas Hutchinson had capitulated and agreed to move the British regiments out of Boston.

In November of 1773, a citizens' group resolved that tea, with its objectionable Townshend duty, should not be landed in Boston. A month later, after futile efforts to get Hutchinson to return the tea ships to England, a

Pews and balcony of Old South Church. Washington inspected the "scene of desolation" from this balcony when he entered Boston in March of 1776.

fateful meeting was held which ended at the docks late on the night of December 16. Led by Sam Adams, and with faces blackened and swinging hatchets, a mob of "Indians" smashed the tea chests of three ships and dumped the contents into the harbor.

Meetings held in the church were inevitably fiery. On one occasion feeling ran so high that when Dr. Joseph Warren, a noted patriot, arrived to give a memorial address on the Boston Massacre, he entered the pulpit through a window to avoid conflict with British officers present.

In March of 1776, the British evacuated Boston for the safer environs of New York. Before they left, Bostonians were shocked to see Old South converted into a riding school for Burgoyne's cavalry. Pews and pulpit were ripped out and used for fuel. When Washington arrived in Boston on the heels of the British, he looked at the shambles left of the Old South Church and expressed surprise that a nation that venerated their own houses of worship should have so desecrated one in the colonies.

The ornate pulpit dates from 1857, but the sounding board above it is thought to be from the colonial period.

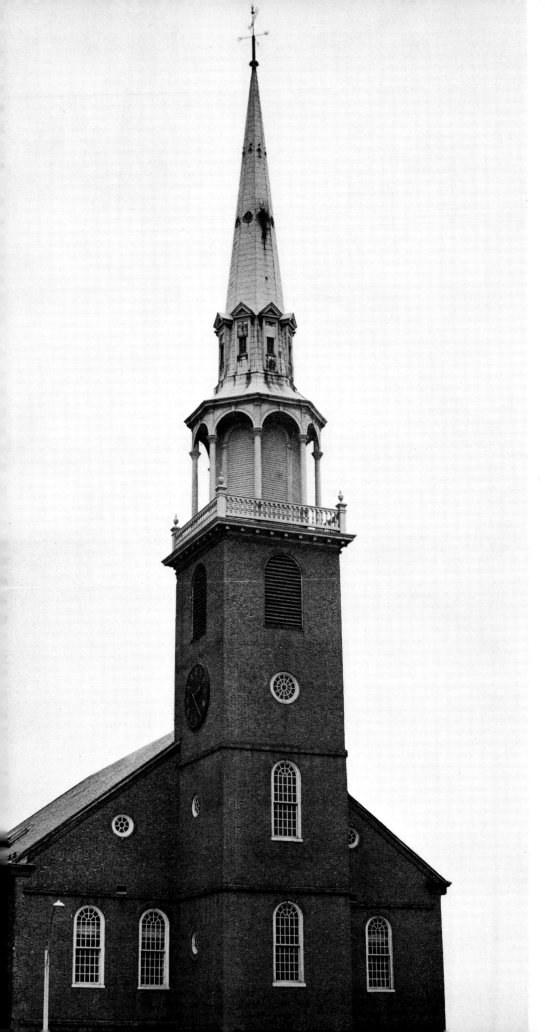

In June of 1876, an auction notice appeared in a Boston paper stating that the purchaser of Old South would have sixty days to remove the remains. "The Spire is covered with copper, and there is a lot of lead on roof and belfry, and the roof is covered with imported old Welch slate." Fortunately, a citizens' group led by Wendell Phillips raised funds to save the church for posterity.

1767

The John Dickinson Home

Dover, Delaware

JOHN Dickinson of Delaware is not as well known as some other figures of the Revolutionary period, yet Jefferson called him one of the "great worthies" and he has been ranked with Franklin and Washington in relative achievements. He was known as the "penman of the Revolution." His "Letters

The Dickinson home stands in a formal garden surrounded by the plantation fields, much as it did two hundred years ago. A fire gutted the house after the war, but it was rebuilt under John Dickinson's supervision in 1806.

The summer kitchen was a work wing. Soap and tallow were made here, as well as sausage.

from a Farmer in Pennsylvania" convinced many people of the justice of the patriot cause, yet he later refused to sign the Declaration of Independence. He abhorred violence, but was one of the few members of the Congress who went on active duty during the war.

Dickinson was raised on the far-reaching family plantation on Jones Neck below Dover, and at fifteen was riding on errands concerning tobacco and tenants for his father. At eighteen he studied law in Philadelphia, then at London's Middle Temple. While practicing law in Philadelphia in 1757, he

This maple desk was presented to John Dickinson when a boy. Even then he was a diligent writer.

*In a second-floor sewing room the window looks out over the formal gardens
and the farm beyond.*

soon became known as a conservative friend of liberty, critical of Crown policy, yet opposed to complete independence. Although he refused to put his name on the Declaration of Independence, he raised a regiment of Pennsylvania militia and went to New Jersey at their head to oppose the enemy there. Later he moved his family back to the mansion near Dover and, in 1777, enlisted as a private in the Delaware militia for a tour of duty. His efforts in collecting arms for the state earned him a brigadier general's commission.

The British occupation of Philadelphia meant hardship for its inhabitants, and Dickinson sent grain, meat, and two hundred cords of firewood for their relief. After he had drafted the Articles of Confederation his estate was hit hard by a raiding party of Loyalists from New York. His home was plundered and all his silver and stores of meat taken. While he was home repairing the damage he was chosen president of Delaware.

John Dickinson's last major contribution was to urge ratification of the new Constitution in 1787. His state signed first, a result of his long work in protecting the rights of small states and convincing them of the need for the Constitution.

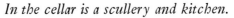

In the cellar is a scullery and kitchen.

This tiny front parlor on the first floor was called the "book room" in John Dickinson's childhood.

Twin bed chambers on the second floor have fireplaces served by the great end chimney.

The exterior of Old State House is little changed since Revolutionary days.

1770

Old State House

Boston, Massachusetts

*T*HE official name for this structure is the Second Boston Town House, the first having burned down in 1711. Here sat a house of representatives elected by the people of the province of Massachusetts Bay. When Bostonians began calling it the "State House," they aroused the ire of Governor Bernard, who thought the colonists were overestimating their authority.

From its earliest days, this building was a center of controversy. Here, in 1761, James Otis challenged the legality of "writs of assistance." These were search warrants issued by the courts in an effort to curb a popular New England habit of avoiding customs duties. The Americans felt that their rights as Englishmen were being violated and that any act of Parliament that infringed upon those rights was void. Otis lost the case but became the leader of the radical wing of the colonists. In 1764, he headed the extralegal Committee of Correspondence formed by Samuel Adams.

Tempers were growing shorter in Boston. The Stamp Act had caused riots in the streets. One snowy night in March of 1770, a mob jeered and taunted a sentry before the Customs House, just below Old State House. He sent for aid and when the redcoats arrived they replied to the abuse by firing into the crowd. British Captain Preston had not ordered them to do so, and the resulting trial was watched by a seething Boston incensed by the five dead and Paul Revere's inflammatory and inaccurate engraving that was sold everywhere. The incredible part of this tragic episode was that patriot leaders John Adams and Josiah Quincy undertook to defend the accused soldiers when lawyers for

The British lion wears a royal crown on the façade of the Old State House.

them could not be found in infuriated Boston. They won an acquittal for all but two, who were convicted of manslaughter, branded on the hand, and released. Both sides were at fault that night.

The first black American to fall before British guns, Crispus Attucks, died here in the snow before Old State House.

James Otis, the most prominent of the speakers for colonial rights who raised their voices in the Old State House, continued his attacks on Crown policy until 1769. He was accosted on the streets of Boston by a Tory commissioner of customs who beat him severely about the head with a cutlass. Though Otis lived until 1783, he was a broken man, his mind unhinged by his injuries. Though unable to sign the Declaration of Independence, no man had earned the right more than he.

This is where James Otis led the fight against the "writs of assistance" and caused John Adams to declare later that here "the child Independence was born."

Extensive changes in later years, when the structure was Boston's City Hall, changed the layout of the second floor considerably. This circular foyer did not exist in colonial times.

An American eagle surveys new Boston from its perch on the Old State House.

Faneuil Hall

Boston, Massachusetts

*T*HIS imposing structure on Dock Square has had a checkered history. It was conceived in controversy when it was offered to Boston as a market house in 1740 by the town's leading merchant, Peter Faneuil. Country farmers and merchants preferred door-to-door peddling and were cool to competitive selling under one roof, but the town merchants outvoted them and Faneuil's offer was accepted.

As completed in 1742, it was a two-story Georgian structure, 40 by 100 feet, with a long meeting hall on the second floor. Fire left it a ruin in 1761, but it was restored by 1763.

Patriot leaders met here regularly until the huge numbers of citizens involved forced frequent adjournments to the more spacious Old South Meeting-House a few blocks away.

In November of 1772, Samuel Adams succeeded in creating here a new

A bold American eagle with the motto "E Pluribus Unum" surmounts the balcony rail above the meeting room.

Paintings of colonial leaders decorate the walls of the meeting room. These are copies, the originals being in the Boston Museum of Fine Arts.

body, without legality in British eyes, called the Committee of Correspondence. This was the forerunner of the First Continental Congress and the first framework for organizing a union of the American colonies.

The hall became a theater for Tories during the seige of Boston. It remained unchanged in appearance until urgent demands for enlarged market space around the turn of the century brought Charles Bullfinch on the scene. He rebuilt the entire structure, tripling its size, adding a third floor, and shifting the cupola to the opposite end.

While its appearance is much changed from colonial days, Faneuil Hall still retains the historic meeting room on the second floor, while busy markets thrive on the ground level.

Peter Faneuil, painted holding a sketch of the original design for his market house.

Faneuil Hall, a meeting place for patriot leaders, was greatly enlarged by the architect Bullfinch in 1806. He also provided rows of barrel-shaped dormers to light the attic space.

1774

Carpenters' Hall

Philadelphia, Pennsylvania

*I*N COLONIAL America, carpenters were also builders and designers. To advance the science of architecture and provide for members of their profession in need, the Carpenters' Company of Philadelphia was organized in 1724. An attractive two-story structure was built for their headquarters in 1770.

Samuel Adams was the prime mover for the Continental Congress that met here in September and October of 1774. He had sent Paul Revere to Philadelphia in May to broach the idea with patriot leaders. Adams was anxious to resolve differences between the southern and New England colonies and so

One of the two ornate fireplaces in the first-floor meeting room.

Situated at the end of a narrow court off Chestnut Street, Carpenters' Hall is unchanged from colonial times.

present a united front to Britain. An early test came when the delegates were offered the assembly room of the State House and rejected it in favor of meeting in Carpenters' Hall.

The deliberations were conducted in secret, the orators of the radical faction—Patrick Henry, Samuel Adams, and others—soon swinging the Congress to their views. It was more than a simple vote for reconciliation or steadfast resistance, however. Over a period of weeks, the gifted writers present—John Adams, John Dickinson, Patrick Henry, John Jay, and Richard Henry Lee—produced a series of papers stating the grievances and rights that must be redressed. This declaration was actually a forerunner of the Declaration of Independence and clarified many goals.

The Congress pledged aid to beleaguered Boston and agreed to a boycott of British goods. They voted to meet again the following May and dissolved the session, their aims accomplished.

From the beginning, the delegates conducted their work with courage and dispatch. Tory sentiment was strong in many of the colonies and a Royalist newspaper in Philadelphia warned that should these rebels choose to meet in Carpenters' Hall, the members of that organization might have their property confiscated and "their necks might be inconveniently lengthened."

One of several wall sconces that date from Revolutionary days in Carpenters' Hall.

This huge chamber was bisected by a long entry hall at the time of the Congress. The meeting was held in this half of the room.

These Windsor armchairs are those actually used by the delegates in 1774.

St. John's Church

Richmond, Virginia

*P*ATRICK HENRY was the second of nine children. An indifferent scholar, he dropped out of school at fifteen. Until he married a neighbor's daughter three years later, he idled away much of his time fishing, riding horses, and playing his fiddle at country dances. His married life was no more settled, he and his wife having no fixed home for several years.

Henry visited Williamsburg when he was twenty-four, and discussed entering law practice with friends. Thomas Jefferson introduced him to a brilliant circle, including George Wythe, Francis Payton, and John Randolph. Henry seemed finally to have a purpose in life. He passed his exams in an incredibly short time and only three years later won the "Parsons Cause" suit. This complicated case established his legal reputation, and his attacks on the Stamp Act in 1765 brought him to the forefront of the Virginia patriots. He served in the Virginia House of Burgesses and at the Continental Congress in 1774.

It was at the Virginia Convention in 1775 that Patrick Henry electrified and unified an uncertain delegation. A strong faction was present that wished to temporize, hoping still for reconciliation with the Crown. Edmund Pendleton and Benjamin Harrison had just urged caution and forebearance when Henry took the floor and made an impassioned plea for liberty. He spoke extemporaneously and his words were only recorded later by his listeners. After a cogent plea for a realistic view of Britain's successive acts against the colonies, he warned that a further delay might find a "British guard stationed in every house." He concluded with these words that swept the convention to a chorus of "ayes" carrying his resolutions:

"It is in vain, Sir, to extenuate the matter. Gentlemen may cry, peace, peace —but there is no peace. The war is actually begun! The next gale that sweeps from the north will bring to our ears the clash of resounding arms! Our brethren are already in the field! Why stand we here idle? What is it that gentlemen wish? What would they have? Is life so dear, or peace so sweet, as to be purchased at the price of chains and slavery? Forbid it, Almighty God! I know not what course others may take, but as for me, give me liberty, or give me death!"

St. John's Church has been altered several times since the Virginia Convention met within its walls in 1775. The tower and belfry were erected after 1830.

Side entrance was the original main entrance to the simple rectangular structure built in 1740.

The transept, or crossing, of the enlarged church was the entire original of the 25-by-40-foot interior.

From this pew, Patrick Henry rose to arouse the delegates with his plea for armed support of the New England colonists.

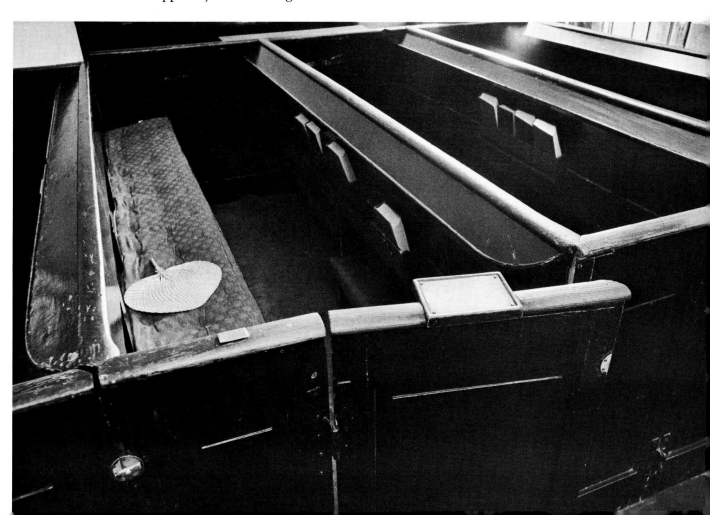

The Paul Revere House

Boston, Massachusetts

BORN and raised in Boston, the melting pot of colonial America, Paul Revere grew up to know the working class and the aristocracy of New England better than most. At his father's side, he learned to work gold and silver. If he had never lifted a finger in political activity, he would still be in the history books as the greatest silversmith of his time in America.

He was nineteen when his father died, too young legally to continue the family smithy. His apprenticeship would run out at twenty-two, and only then could he have official sanction to call himself a master silversmith. His mother could run the business, however, so he calmly and unofficially stepped into his father's shoes and trade prospered.

The skilled artisans of Boston were acquainted with the leading figures of

The house Paul Revere lived in [ ] been restored to its original [ ] pearance in the seventeenth c[ ] tury. It was built soon after [ ] great Boston fire of 1676. T[ ] second-story overhang is typi[ ] of homes of the period.

The kitchen ell at the rear of Revere's house. The well pump has been restored to its original design.

the day. Revere had a sound education by his fifteenth year and could converse on current issues with the alumni of Harvard. He soon knew Samuel Adams, John Hancock, and the rising, handsome Dr. Joseph Warren. Revere was a dedicated patriot, not given to imaginative ideals and visionary plans, but ready at a moment to carry out any arduous tasks assigned by rebel leaders.

He was married twice and had sixteen children altogether. In 1764, smallpox swept Boston and soon the Revere family was behind locked doors, the "infected" flag hanging out, to await the worst. All survived their attacks, but later several children died in infancy.

Revere managed his heavy silver trade, the apprentices under him, and a houseful of children and relatives, yet found time to be deeply involved in every rebel cause fermenting in Boston. He was soon the most trusted of

The ceiling of the large room is spanned by huge beams. The second-floor rafters and floor are restored.

couriers, taking messages as far as Philadelphia for Sam Adams and James Otis.

One message, destined to herald a new nation, brought him, booted and spurred, to his back door (to avoid the crowded streets and Tory eyes) on a night in April of 1775.

The leaded glass window and the iron, bolt-studded door reflect the seventeenth-century origin of Revere's house. It is thought that Revere left for his famous ride by way of the better concealed rear door.

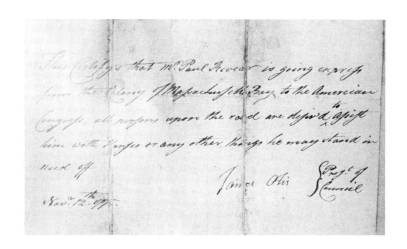

A courier's pass dated November 12, 1775, and signed by James Otis reads: "This certifys that Mr. Paul Revere is going express from the Colony of Massachusetts Bay to the American Congress, all persons upon the road are desired to assist him with horses or any other things he may stand in need of."

A coattail chair in the large room of Revere's house. A gentleman could sit in such a chair without the split tails of his coat becoming crushed.

The second-floor bed chamber has been restored as it was in Revere's lifetime.

Fireplace and oven in the kitchen ell.

The fireplace in the large room. This multipurpose room served for dining, as a parlor, and also as a connecting hall that linked the kitchen ell and rear entrance to the winding stairs leading to the upper floor.

Wooden downspouts and overhang of an upper floor are typical of seventeenth-century houses. The carved pendant was a popular decorative device.

1775

Old North Church

Boston, Massachusetts

*T*HE NEWS of the secret march out of Boston by British troops had slipped out. They would go to Concord and seize powder and arms rumored to be stored there by the colonists. Dr. Joseph Warren and Paul Revere arranged for the twin signal lanterns to be placed in the belfry of Old North Church. Almost three hundred feet above the ground, they would be seen by patriots on the far side of the Charles River and alert them to the redcoats coming out of Boston. Where Warren got the closely guarded details of General Gage's secret plan is not known, but some historians suspect that it was from the general's American-born and intensely patriotic wife. Boston was riddled with secret spy organizations run by patriots, and not much skill was required to deduce that the British would move their troops by water when they openly launched a flotilla of ships' boats and tied them up near the men-of-war in the Charles River. The target, Concord, was no secret at all, and a special committee had already been assigned by the patriots to watch out for the safety of Sam Adams and John Hancock, presently staying nearby in Lexington.

After arranging for the lanterns at the Old North Church, Revere and William Dawes departed to warn the countryside and alert Lexington and Concord. Dawes took the longer route and, eluding British soldiers, warned Roxbury, Cambridge, and Menotomy, ending his ride at Lexington.

Revere barely avoided two British horsemen, and after having the Medford company of Minutemen turn out, he arrived at Lexington shortly before

The steeple of Old North Church was a landmark for seamen, so appreciated by English merchants of Honduras that they donated to its construction.

Historians are in doubt as to whether Captain John Pulling, Jr., or Robert Newman actually carried the warning lanterns aloft, but this is where the climb began. The stairs wind up the tower and, before reaching the wooden portion of the belfry, pass this circular window that reveals the great thickness of the sturdy brick walls.

The stairs grow increasingly narrower and more cramped as they approach the belfry of Old North Church.

Dawes. Alarm guns were sounding throughout the countryside and the two couriers, joined by a Dr. Samuel Prescott, now headed for Concord, alerting homes along the road. They were suddenly accosted at pistol point by several British officers. Dawes escaped in the dark, returning to Lexington. Prescott, who knew the adjoining fields intimately, jumped his horse over a stone wall and escaped. Paul Revere headed for a woods, but six more British appeared and forced him to dismount.

Surprisingly, after marching Revere and three previously captured patriots back toward Lexington, the British cut the bridles of their mounts and released the rebel prisoners. Revere had alarmed them with a tale of five hundred Minutemen assembling, and they appeared to value his horse more than his person. They took his mount and left him with a sorry nag that a British sergeant had been riding. The fine animal that took Revere on his famous ride never was found by the Americans, that night or later.

Paul Revere was well acquainted with Old North Church long before he directed the hanging of the famous lanterns that April night. As a boy of fifteen, Revere formed a guild of youthful friends and obtained permission to peal regularly the eight bells hanging in the tower. He was a Congregationalist and not a member of this oldest church in Boston, but his attachments ran deep and he was seen often in old age in the pew of his oldest son, who had joined Christ Church.

Architecturally, this beautiful structure is made of brick, laid in immensely thick walls. Its interior is surprisingly light and airy, with a huge window over the altar. It clearly shows the influence of that remarkable skyline of churches erected in London by Christopher Wren. The first wooden steeple raised atop the 100-foot high brick tower was 191 feet tall, a prodigious achievement for colonial craftsmen in 1740. A wind storm in 1804 took it down, and a recent hurricane toppled its successor. The present tower is an authentic copy of the colonial design.

It is rare when legend, beauty, and historical significance combine, but Old North Church is a moving example of such a landmark.

The organ of Christ Church, or Old North, is unusual in that it was made in America and not in England. Thomas Johnston of Boston built the case shown here. The actual organ he built around 1760 has been replaced several times, but the current restoration is similar in tone to the eighteenth-century original.

One of four polychromed wooden statues of cherubim that decorate the organ loft. Destined for a French church in Quebec, they became a privateer's booty. Being a member of Christ Church, the ship owner donated them to the congregation in 1746.

The simple lines of the acoustical sounding board that hangs above the pulpit harmonize with the soaring lines of the great window.

The interior of Old North Church is distinguished by these brass chandeliers. They are surmounted by a dove of peace and were first lighted in 1724. The high box pews were arranged to prevent cold drafts from chilling the worshippers, who shared a family foot-warmer in each pew.

1775

The Hancock-Clarke House

Lexington, Massachusetts

*I*N THE small village of Lexington, consisting of just over a hundred families, the Reverend Jonas Clarke was a powerful influence. He had been educated by Edward Holyoke at Harvard, and formed his convictions about political freedom from him and the humanist teachings of John Locke.

Clarke had arrived in Lexington in 1755 to take over the parsonage of John Hancock the elder, who had died at eighty-two years of age after serving as minister to the Lexington flock for fifty-four years. In the next twenty years Clarke became not only the religious leader of the community but a political thinker known and respected far beyond Lexington. His detailed attack upon the Stamp Act was a model of radical colonial thought on the subject. His busy pen turned out sermons by the thousands and scores of papers on the political questions of the day. The rather cramped parsonage house, built by Grandfather John Hancock in 1698, was packed with Clarke's active family of ten children. Clarke's wife was a granddaughter of old John Hancock; in the spring a guest arrived who was also a grandchild of the older Hancock. This was John Hancock, chairman of the Committee of Safety and president of the Provincial Congress. With him, as poor as Hancock was rich, was Samuel Adams, the political genius of the Revolutionary movement. This illustrious company delighted Jonas Clarke, and the exchange of views of the city attitudes toward the British and the feelings of the country folk were beneficial to all.

By April, it was plain that Hancock and Adams had better not return to

The front room of the 1734 addition to the Clarke parsonage.

Boston when the Concord session of the Provincial Congress they were attending was over. General Gage had been ordered to arrest and bring in these two firebrands of rebellion, and quickly.

When Paul Revere pounded up to the Clarke parsonage that April evening near midnight, he found the house guarded by ten Minutemen and ablaze with light. Only the youngest of the ten children were asleep, while their elders discussed the latest rumors. Told that the regulars were out and on their way, impetuous Hancock wanted to wait on the green with Captain Parker and his Minutemen, but Sam Adams convinced him he would be of

*At a table before this fireplace, Sam Adams and John Hancock discussed
political questions into the night with the Reverend Jonas Clarke.*

no use if arrested and imprisoned. Finally, a carriage was brought and the
party left for the concealment of a nearby woods. Revere was asked to pick
up a trunk packed with incriminating records of the Committee of Safety
that Hancock had left at Buckman's Tavern on Lexington Green. Although
Paul Revere undoubtedly heard the first shots fired on the green, he was
struggling to carry off Hancock's unwieldy chest several houses away and
was unaware of just what was happening. With the Clarke house now free of
its guests, the scene of action shifted to a few score men gathered at the tavern
on Lexington Green.

Clarke wrote his sermons and kept the meticulous journals of his farm at this desk in the second-floor front room.

The two-story structure at left was the original parsonage before the wing adjoining was added at a later date.

1775

Buckman's Tavern

Lexington, Massachusetts

*I*N 1775, Buckman's hostelry was an old, established landmark, having been built in 1690. John Buckman, a Lexington Minuteman, was the owner. The Minuteman company was accustomed to retiring to the Buckman taproom after their training sessions on the green. In those days, the village tavern was also the lodging place for travelers. News went ! y horseback and the tavern was the discussion center of the village.

In this large clapboard structure, small rooms were provided on the third floor for servants, while other guests roomed on the first and second floors. The large rooms of the first floor were the taproom itself, a large kitchen, and

The massive Buckman Tavern is virtually unchanged since that chilly dawn of April 19, 1775, when a war started at its doorstep.

This room was reserved for lady travelers. The fireplace is opposite the one serving the taproom.

a room where the ladies might visit apart from the men who crowded the taproom. All the larger rooms had ample fireplaces opening off a huge central chimney.

The men of Lexington gathered at the tavern after Revere's midnight alarm. Captain John Parker, a sound, sensible man and former Indian fighter, was their elected commander. His company numbered about 130 men on the green that night. After standing about in the chill air for an hour, and having no definite word of the whereabouts of the British, Parker dismissed his men, to assemble at the beat of the drum. Although many scouts were sent out, the redcoats caught most of them and with scarcely twenty minutes warning, the alarm came at four-thirty in the morning. The British were coming! Men poured out of the tavern where they had been dozing before the fire. Others came from nearby houses. Muskets were hastily borrowed for those who had none, and the scanty supply of powder and ball was issued.

From this moment, as sixteen-year-old Billy Diamond beat the assembly roll on his drum, events would move beyond the control or wishes of both sides.

This view of the room reserved for the ladies shows a guest bedroom at the rear.

A spacious kitchen behind the taproom served the tavern's guests.

The kitchen fireplace with the adjoining oven.

In this taproom, the Lexington Minutemen awaited the call to arms. The serving bar is at right.

At Lexington Green

*W*HILE the early morning sun shone on the bayonets of the British column approaching the triangular green, Captain John Parker formed those men who were ready and present into two thin lines, numbering about seventy-seven Minutemen in all. This was an apparent change in plans, since he had earlier cautioned his men not to "meddle with" and "not to be discovered" by the British. Everyone knew that the English meant to seize the arms at Concord, and it is strange that the colonials thought six or eight hundred of the King's soldiers would march past a handful of rebel militia and not attempt to disarm them.

During the night, Captain Parker probably conferred with Hancock and Sam Adams. Reverend Clarke was also Parker's close and good friend. If any suggestions were made by the patriot leaders, Parker would have undoubtedly carried them out. Sam Adams, master of the Boston mobs, might have desired the confrontation between the Minutemen and the Royal troops. Historians have conjectured much about what the Minutemen thought to accomplish by this show of arms. A feeling of pride in their rights and a need to display their defiance of the hated occupying army were probably the chief motives. Few thought that the British would seriously molest them. When the order rang out to "Lay down your arms, you damned rebels, and disperse!" they stood in surprise, and even after Captain Parker ordered them to disband, they moved slowly and without discarding their muskets. That order had clearly not been anticipated and they automatically carried their guns with them. All might yet have ended without bloodshed if the British had been cool, disciplined, and dispassionate troops. These soldiers, however, had been on the move since ten o'clock of the previous evening. They had waded through the swampy banks of the Charles, stood around wet and cold waiting for provisions they did not need, and then marched about ten miles to Lexington. They knew they were in hostile country and despised the rebels who had brought them on this miserable errand. When they were yet out of sight, they heard Billy Diamond's drum roll. Their leader, Major Pitcairn of the Royal Marines, recognized it as an assembly signal. He halted the column and had the troops load with powder and ball. They were keyed up to a fighting pitch by the time they saw the rebel ranks.

Parker was now urging his men to break ranks, to disband. Pitcairn was impatiently cursing the rebels' slowness in complying. Someone fired—from a window, a stone wall, an officer's pistol, a redcoat musket, a rebel musket. Every theory has been advanced. No one will ever know who fired that first shot, but it triggered the redcoats' smoldering fury. A British volley went high; a ragged reply came from the dazed Americans. A second row of redcoats fired into the patriots' sagging ranks. Eight dropped to stay; others fell wounded. Jonas Parker, cousin to Captain Parker, fired even as Major Pitcairn was screaming at his men to cease fire. Parker was hit, staggered, and yet stood his ground as he had been ordered to earlier and was reloading his musket when he was bayoneted, his son at his side.

The British charged, and men went running into Buckman's Tavern for cover; others leaped nearby stone walls. Among the men in that line who returned the British fire was Prince Estabrook, a Negro slave who later won his freedom by gallant service in the Continental army.

Most of the rebels were family men over thirty, a few quite a bit older, one of sixty-three. Twelve teen-agers were there, and eight fathers with their sons at their sides. Young Jonathan Harrington was struck in the chest by a musket ball. He crawled to the steps of his house on the edge of the common, and died at the feet of his wife and eight-year-old son.

The sun was now fully up. There were jubilant cheers and a victory volley from the British, while the women of Lexington tended the wounded amid their dead on the Green. Soon the enemy column reformed and, music playing, departed for Concord. They were due for some surprises before this long day was over.

*On this drum in the morning light of April 19, 1775, sixteen-year-old Billy
Diamond beat the assembly roll, calling the Minutemen to arms.*

LINE OF THE MINUTE MEN
APRIL 19, 1775

STAND YOUR GROUND
DONT FIRE UNLESS FIRED UPON
BUT IF THEY MEAN TO HAVE A WAR
LET IT BEGIN HERE

CAPTAIN PARKER

One end of Parker's line stood here, and here Jonathan Harrington fell, mortally wounded. He crawled to the steps of his house, shown here at the edge of the common, and died at the feet of his wife and son.

There was little to choose from in weapons—the British "Brown Bess" musket (above) against an American gun (below). Effective range was about seventy-five yards for either weapon. Most of the arms used by the colonists were made in France.

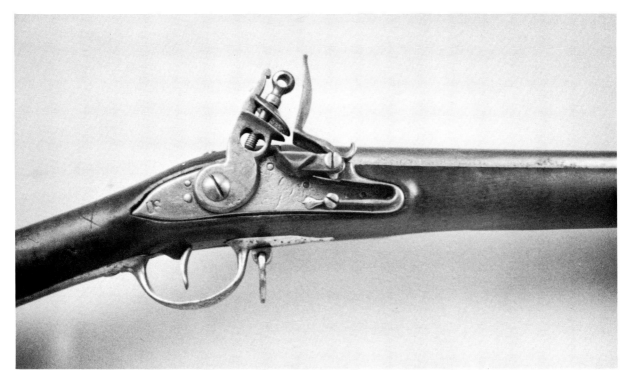

At Concord Bridge and on Battle Road

*W*HILE Major Pitcairn, after sharply reprimanding his men to heed orders, marched his column off to Concord, Captain John Parker was rounding up his scattered company from fields and houses where they had sensibly fled the British bayonets.

Not all the action that morning was in Lexington and Concord. Offstage, thousands waited in the wings for their chance to perform. Colonel Conant and friends had been alerting the countryside since the lanterns went up in Old North Church. Lynn, north of Boston, was aroused at dawn. By daylight, Danvers, Tewksbury, Reading, Woburn, and Acton, Billerica, and Andover had all been warned. Some towns were thirty and forty miles away, but they made ready. Church bells could be heard in the still country air from village to village and a telegraph of pealing bells rolled the long-awaited alarm across the colony of Massachusetts Bay.

The young Dr. Prescott, who had made good his escape earlier by leaping his horse over a stone fence, brought the alert to Concord at 1:00 A.M. and soon three companies of Minutemen were turned out. The most urgent task was to complete the concealment of arms and powder started the day before. Furrows were hurriedly plowed in a field and small cannon and muskets were turned under. Flints, balls, and cartridges were concealed in barrels that were stored in attics under piles of feathers.

About seven o'clock, the British column appeared, approaching Concord. Several companies of Minutemen and militia took position on the ridges

The Minuteman farmer, on hearing the alarm gun or pealing church bell, put aside the plow and left for the scene of action, musket in hand. (A detail of the statue by Daniel Chester French.)

overlooking the road, but seeing the size of the enemy force and the flankers approaching to clear their ground, they wisely withdrew. Reinforcements were constantly arriving: 38 came from Acton; Bedford sent an early detachment, 79 strong; Lincoln, 62. Hundreds responded to the sound of the church bells ringing the alarm. Colonel James Barrett, commanding the area's militia, drew the forces he could get word to back to the high ground above the village. Their way into Concord unopposed, the British entered and searched the houses for arms. What little they found—two cannon and five hundred pounds of musket balls, plus several gun carriages—they disposed of so poorly that much was salvaged later. They burned the gun carriages, set fire to the courthouse and a smithy, then changed their minds and extinguished the blaze.

Colonel Barrett and his officers decided that the town was being put to the

Swollen waters of the Concord River overflow its banks at the site of the "rude bridge that arched the flood."

Two British soldiers who died at the battle of Concord bridge were buried by the Americans where they fell.

torch and a force of some four hundred marched to its rescue. They ordered the men to fire only if fired upon, an order everyone was using that morning with little success.

British Colonel Smith, a portly gentleman who kept the pace of his column down to his own slow gait, barely got to Concord bridge in time to confront the Americans. The British opened fire and only when several of the militia had been wounded and two Minutemen of the Acton company (Captain Isaac Davis and Abner Hosmer) fell dead did the Americans reply. Their volley killed three and wounded nine of the enemy. The redcoats fled back into the village in disarray. The Americans removed their dead and wounded and wandered off, failing to realize that the bridge should be secured.

An incident occurred after both sides had left the scene that had important repercussions later. A farm boy of about thirteen was running to cross the bridge, presumably to join the patriot group, when a severely wounded redcoat, apparently left for dead in the ditch, staggered toward him. Thinking he was being attacked, the youth dispatched the soldier with a blow of a hatchet he was carrying. When the British unit under Captain Parsons recrossed the bridge to join the troops in town, they found the soldier's body

A replica of the original bridge where patri

...ilitia confronted British regulars at Concord.

A group of Minutemen were pursued to the doorway of this house in Menotomy by a British flanking party. The owner, a fifty-eight-year-old cripple named Jason Russell, had taken his family to safety and returned to guard his home. Here he was shot and bayoneted to death. The redcoats used their bayonets savagely in the house, slaying eleven Minutemen. Eight survivors fled to the cellar where they defied the British to come down. One tried and was slain; the others fled.

and concluded that the Americans were scalping their captives. This report spread among the troops and may have been responsible for some of the excesses committed during the running battle later.

The British finally decided that their mission in Concord had been accomplished and departed about noon. A delay of two hours and the necessity of taking the same road back to Lexington was to cost them heavily. During those two hours, patriots had been on their way from dozens of towns, eager to avenge Lexington, though few knew just what had occurred.

The first ambush was at Meriam's Corner. The British had flankers out, but the Americans knew the ground. Captain Parker's company was back to strength and struck savagely in Lincoln township. By the time the British reached Lexington, they were in near rout. Had this been the only body of

In the course of the fighting, Major Pitcairn was thrown from his horse. The animal ran to rebel forces who acquired these dress pistols from the saddle holsters. They were later presented to General Israel Putnam.

Amos Locke carried this musket and powder horn when he stood in the ranks
of the Minutemen on Lexington Green that fateful morning. He survived the
British bullets and bayonet charges to fire his musket over this wall many
times later that day.

British troops in the field, victory for the colonists would have been certain. But General Gage had organized a relief party under General Percy of about one thousand, and although they were much delayed, their arrival saved Smith's battered command. From two o'clock on, the combined column retired toward Boston and the safety of the guns of the fleet. The retreat was savage; looting and burning became the normal course and men found in roadside houses were slain by the British. In Menotomy, forty patriots and forty English died in hand-to-hand combat.

The factor that counted most for the British was the cool, skillful command of General Earl Percy. He used his two six-pounders to intimidate the rebels, who were almost totally unused to artillery. The Americans were hurt by the absence of a single command.

Before the day was over, 3,700 patriots took part in the war along the road to Boston. Over 80,000 shots were exchanged and the American casualties were 95, compared to 273 for the British. At several points, an additional five hundred fresh Minutemen might have enabled the patriots to close the road and force surrender. This victory, however, would have proved costly. To send out 1,800 of the King's army and have them return beaten was one thing; to send them out and never see them return would have precipitated a savage repercussion, too swift to allow the new Continental army to come into being.

In this room delegates from the thirteen colonies cut the ties with Britain when they signed the Declaration of Independence, using this silver inkstand.

1776

Independence Hall

Philadelphia, Pennsylvania

*T*HIS State House for the colony of Pennsylvania got its popular name from the adoption within its walls of the Declaration of Independence in July of 1776. The year before, the Second Continental Congress had met here. Fighting had already broken out at Lexington and Concord, and talk of reconciliation was a thing of the past. This Congress made plans to raise an army

Benjamin Franklin once pondered aloud as to whether this sun carved on the speaker's chair of the Pennsylvania State House was rising or setting. After the adoption of the Constitution, he declared it was certainly a rising sun.

The Liberty Bell.

and appointed George Washington, a planter of Virginia, to be its leader.

Easily the most famous artifact of American freedom is the Liberty Bell, preserved here in Independence Hall. Its inscription, "Proclaim Liberty Throughout All The Land Unto All The Inhabitants Thereof," has no direct association with the Declaration of Independence, however. It was originally ordered cast in London to celebrate the fiftieth anniversary of William Penn's Charter of Privileges. Cracked when first rung in Philadelphia, the bell was successfully recast by Pass and Stow. It was used frequently until it cracked irreparably when tolling the funeral of Chief Justice John Marshall in 1835. During the Revolution it was carted to Allentown and hidden when the fall of Philadelphia to the British was imminent. A little-known twin bell, cast at the same time, hangs in a Mount Vernon, New York, church. This bell, also buried during the Revolution, is known as the Freedom Bell.

Congress met for ten years in one wing of Independence Hall and the Supreme Court in another. Both great documents that were to guide the destiny of the nation were forged in this structure. The Declaration of Independence, written largely by Thomas Jefferson, was adopted and signed here, and in 1787, the Federal Constitutional Convention met here. Men toiled four months and produced our Constitution, reconciling regional differences and providing for a democratic government.

Another view of the Liberty Bell.

The rear court of Independence Hall.

1776

Conference House

Staten Island, New York

WHILE the historic signing of the Declaration of Independence was taking place in Philadelphia the first week in July, Lord Howe occupied Staten Island. On August 27, he drove the Continental army from Long Island. Only a brilliant effort by Washington enabled the entire force to escape capture. Pursued across New Jersey, the rebels tried to hold a disintegrating army together. The British felt that surely the Congress in Philadelphia would now be happy to sue for peace. Accordingly, Admiral Lord Howe, brother of General Howe, invited the Americans to send envoys for a peace conference under a safe conduct guarantee.

Benjamin Franklin, Edward Rutledge, and John Adams were selected to attend, and they rode overland by horseback to Perth Amboy on the Jersey shore. A barge manned by redcoats met them and ferried them across Raritan Bay to the tip of Staten Island. Lord Howe welcomed them and the delegation filed between ranks of soldiers, who looked, according to John Adams, "as fierce as ten furies."

They were conducted to the old manor house of the Billopp family that overlooked the bay and the talks began. Franklin advised Howe of the signing of the Declaration of Independence in July, and declared a willingness to discuss peace terms under the condition that the colonies were independent of Britain. This was the key point that Howe could not agree to, so little progress was made. Lord Howe expressed great distress that he would be forced to take severe measures again the rebels. Franklin replied that the

The Billopp house was built around 1700 and was occupied by Christopher Billopp during the Revolution. A devoted Tory, he moved to New Brunswick after the war.

This ground-floor dining room was the scene of the peace talks.

Americans would lessen his suffering by taking the utmost care of themselves.

The talks ended as civilly as they had begun, and Lord Howe escorted the committee back to his barge for the return trip to the Jersey shore. Benjamin Franklin indulged his wry sense of humor in debarking by endeavoring to tip the sailors. Offering them a handful of gold and silver served a useful purpose, he explained later; the British would be aware that there was hard money in the colonies, and the risk was negligible, since their discipline would not allow them to accept it.

The talks served to prove, finally, that to be free and independent, the colonials would have to win their cause on the battlefield.

A second-floor bedroom of the Billopp house.

The first-floor front room opposite the conference room is the parlor.

A smaller second-floor bedroom is maintained as a Franklin memorial.

The cellar was paved with brick brought over as ships' ballast from Holland and was the original site of the great kitchen. (The brick shown was reproduced by the original maker for the restoration.) An arched vault, 24 feet long, in the far wall may have led to a tunnel used as a means of escape from attack by Indians.

The Gunboat Philadelphia

*A*SIDE from seizing British coastal shipping and shuttling diplomatic agents across the Atlantic, the naval highlights of the war were the successful ventures of John Paul Jones off the British Isles. During the Revolution the most significant feats of seamanship were accomplished in small boats, however, not in frigates. The brilliant, erratic, and later traitorous Benedict Arnold quite possibly saved the Revolutionary cause with a hastily built fleet on the waters of Lake Champlain.

British strategy in 1776 was simple and logical. If the colonies could be cut in two by a thrust from Canada to the Hudson River valley, the rebel forces could be easily defeated. Accordingly, the Royal Governor of Canada, Sir Guy Carleton, mounted an invasion. His vital target was recapture of Fort Ticonderoga, by the autumn of 1776.

Utensils and brick hearth on the Philadelphia, *one of the gunboats involved in the fighting on Lake Champlain.*

This 24-pound shot holed the Philadelphia below the water line and caused the loss of the boat.

Fortunately, the Continental army anticipated such a move and General Benedict Arnold was rushing to completion a fleet of gunboats by August of 1776. Carpenters and shipwrights were sent to Lake Champlain from the New England seaports by the Congress, and they were soon shaping the local oak and pine into a rude naval fleet.

Carleton's thrust had to wait while his navy commander, Captain Thomas Pringle, also built a squadron to sweep the lake clear of rebels. His ships were larger and there were more of them. When the British finally moved down the lake on October 11, shepherding the transports necessary for moving the invasion army, he found Arnold's squadron deployed to meet him. A savage exchange raged throughout the day. Pringle overtook the survivors of the Continental fleet and, though sustaining heavy damage, sank them all in the next two days. It was almost November when his force reached Fort Ticonderoga, however, and the victory proved to be a hollow one. His cannon shot spent, and the season late, he withdrew to St. John's.

The value of Arnold's bold delaying action only became apparent a year later when Burgoyne's army was forced to surrender at Saratoga. The colonies remained intact and the threat to cut them in two was never again as severe.

The Philadelphia *was stoutly built of oak, with a length of 57 feet and a beam of 17 feet. With only one mast, she depended on the muscle power of her 45-man crew at the sweep oars.*

Heaviest gun carried was this 12-pounder mounted on a slide carriage in the bow.

1776

The Thompson-Neely House

Washington Crossing, Pennsylvania

*T*HE WINTER of 1776 found Washington leading a ragged, hungry, and discouraged army. Keeping just one jump ahead of Cornwallis, Washington was probably saved by the casual attitude given to his pursuit by General Howe. That worthy was having a fine time in snug New York and awaited the collapse of the Continental army with confident boredom.

Approaching the Delaware, Washington took great care to secure all boats for miles up and down the river. He spent scarce hard money to do so, to insure the delay of the British. On the Pennsylvania side, near McKonkey's ferry, several stone houses were requisitioned to shelter his staff officers. In one of these homes Washington met with his staff to plan the attack on Trenton, to begin on Christmas night of 1776.

The house was owned by the Thompson and Neely families and was situated on a ridge above the swift and icy Delaware, a short distance upstream from the ferry crossing. In its rooms were quartered eighteen-year-old Lieutenant James Monroe, (later President), Captain William Washington, General Lord Stirling (his title referred to a questionable earldom in Scotland), and Captain James Moore. This last young officer was ill when the party arrived and, despite the efforts of his comrades, died on Christmas Day. Captain Washington and Lieutenant Monroe survived the battle at Trenton, but suffered wounds in capturing a British cannon that threatened the advance.

Before this fireplace in the "great room," Washington and his staff planned the assault on Trenton.

Where Freedom Grew

Like many stone country houses of the region, the Thompson-Neely house was added to over the decades. The great room, or kitchen, was the earliest part, built in 1702 by John Pidcock. Robert Thompson added the two-story west end. Over the years, this landmark has become known as "The House of Decision," an appropriate name for the daring attack planned there, which revitalized the sinking cause of the rebellion.

This stone was erected over the grave of their twenty-four-year-old son, James Moore, by his parents.

This west end of the Thompson-Neely house appears as it did in Washington's time. The east end was added about 1788.

The Battle of Trenton

GENERAL Howe formally closed out the military campaign of 1776 on December 14 with a self-satisfied directive announcing the abject flight of the rebel army across Jersey into Pennsylvania. Troops were to quarter for the winter and stand ready in the unlikely event that the beaten Continentals should attempt an attack.

Washington was in dire straits, indeed. The situation looked so bleak that Congress turned over all control of the military to him, and fled to Baltimore. His Continental army comprised some five or six thousand men. Other units were too far away to help if Howe had elected to cross the Delaware and force a fight. December 31 was looming ahead, and on that day most enlistments would expire and men would leave for the firesides of home. Only 1,400 would be left, a skeleton army of sick and well alike.

While still miles from the Delaware, Washington sent trusted couriers ahead. Every boat to be found was to be bought or "borrowed," and the Jersey bank left bare. The British arrived hot on the heels of the Americans, but appeared willing to wait for the expected freeze-over of the Delaware, rather than assemble rafts to cross after them.

Establishing his men in makeshift huts in the wooded ridges of the Pennsylvania side, Washington sat down with his staff and worked out a complicated and daring plan to strike a blow at the British before his army evaporated. Oblivious to the rising toll of sickness, he planned an operation

The McKonkey ferryhouse, where Washington rested briefly as his troops
were being ferried to the New Jersey side of the Delaware.

Rear view of the McKonkey ferryhouse.

from which there could be no retreat. "Victory or Death" was to be the watchword, and all would hang on its success.

In the gloom of mid-December, a pamphlet printed in Philadelphia was circulated to the troops, and its words made them aware of why they were there: "These are the times that try men's souls. The Summer soldier and the sunshine Patriot will, in this crisis, shrink from the service of their country; but he that stands it *now*, deserves the love and thanks of man and woman . . ."

These electrifying words of Tom Paine, written on a drumhead by the light of a campfire during the Jersey retreat, were felt and believed by the patriot soldiers. The staff who gathered around the table of the Thompson-Neely house were among the stalwarts of the Revolution: Colonel Henry Knox, a Boston bookseller who in his twenties would become a master of artillery warfare; Major General John Sullivan, a wealthy New England lawyer; General Nathanael Greene, a Rhode Island blacksmith. Doctors and fishermen, farmers and merchants had survived defeat after defeat, learning the game of war in the cruelest fashion.

The dining room of the McKonkey ferryhouse provided refreshments for travelers.

Washington is said to have warmed himself before this fire while waiting for his troops to cross at McKonkey's ferry.

The final plan was adopted on December 24. The target was Trenton, and the time was to be dawn of December 26. The particular day was chosen partly because patriot spy John Honeyman had brought word of extensive Christmas celebrations planned by the Hessians, and partly because time was running out for Washington's dwindling forces.

Three separate divisions would cross the Delaware: a force under Colonel Cadwalader would cross near Bristol and engage a British force at Mount Holly, purely as a diversion. A smaller force of seven hundred under General Ewing would cross to cut off an escape route from Trenton. The major force would cross at McKonkey's ferry below the camp and proceed through nine miles of woods and farms to the village of Trenton. Washington would personally lead this force of 2,400 picked men. Each of his staff officers would lead a contingent of his own men, and Colonel Knox was to provide artillery support with eighteen fieldpieces.

All these units assembled on Christmas Day and began embarking as darkness fell. The Marblehead fishermen of Colonel Glover's regiment were asked to repeat that magic night on Long Island when they had spirited the army away from certain capture. Here, their craft were Durham boats, iron ore carriers, built to carry heavy loads but unwieldy and difficult to load over their pointed sterns. The swift current, the dark clouds that covered the full moon, the grinding sweep of huge ice floes, all conspired to prolong the crossing. Thomas Rodney later said it was "as severe a night" as he had ever seen. At eleven o'clock a hail storm broke, and icy sleet poured upon the poorly clad troops huddled in the boats or crowded along the frozen bank. The men who could master the seas off the Grand Banks struggled and finally mastered the treacherous Delaware. The cannon, horses, and all the men, were finally assembled on the Jersey side.

The difficulty of the passage had destroyed the timetable, however. It was not midnight with five safe, dark hours to reach Trenton, but after four in

*ore heavily wooded
n, this lane is where
ashington's men began
 nine-mile march to
enton.*

the morning when the march began. Into the forest of black oak and hickory the men followed a rutted trail slippery with ice and snow. Many were shod only with rags bound around their bleeding feet. Reports soon reached Washington that the flintlocks could not fire because they were iced with sleet. His reply was to fix bayonets and continue. Some of the veterans had carefully wrapped their muskets and would have dry powder when they needed it.

Normally, Hessian patrols would have been out and, on the flat open farmland, would have spotted Washington's advance. This morning, for some reason, they were cancelled. The twin columns rapidly flanking the village were seen only by a picket on the Pennington Road at eight o'clock in the morning. The enemy guard turned out, but fled before the American's ruthless bayonet charge.

At the same moment, Sullivan and his men arrived on the river road and drove the enemy into the town. The surprised Hessians responded rapidly, but the Continentals were faster. Six fieldpieces were trained down Queen and King streets where the Hessians sought to assemble and did terrible damage. Colonel Johann Rall, a cocky Hessian who had nothing but contempt for the American "farmers," desperately tried to form a defense, but the Americans were everywhere. The icy rain falling made the muskets useless and the fighting became a rushing, clubbing, stabbing contest. Rall fell wounded and died the following day. The night before he had been so deep in a card game he had refused to see a Tory farmer who came to his door. A note the man left, warning of the attack, was crumpled and unread in Rall's pocket when he died.

Four thousand men milled in the streets and yards and swarmed through the houses, until in two hours the last resistance collapsed. The last group of Hessians fleeing ran head-on into General St. Clair's brigade. The Americans joyfully fired a volley over their heads before capturing them.

Washington accomplished this incredible feat of arms without either of the other two supporting divisions. Ewing and Cadwalader both declared the crossing was impossible and failed in their objectives. The men under them struggled over in the hundreds, but were ordered back when the fieldpieces could not be brought over as well.

Many battles of the Revolution have been called the turning point of the war. None more aptly fits that description than the capture of Trenton. It is equally true that only Washington would have dared to do it. With retreat cut off by the raging river, he believed his men could do the impossible and they did. A crack regiment of Hessians was destroyed, almost a thousand prisoners taken as well as six cannon. Over one hundred Hessians were casualties, with but four Americans wounded. With the fleeing enemy alerting the nearby garrison at Bordentown, Washington hastened to recross the Delaware to safety. The snow storm worsened and the return trip was even more difficult. While the enemy failed to kill one American in the battle, it is said that three soldiers were taken out of the boats, frozen to death, on the Pennsylvania side.

View of the Delaware from Bowman's Hill, looking toward the site of Washington's crossing at the narrow bend.

The Old Ferry Inn on the Pennsylvania side of the Delaware. Built in 1757, it was added to after the war. Twenty-three captured Hessian officers were kept here briefly, following the battle of Trenton.

An authentic replica of a Durham iron ore boat. Partially decked over, it drew only two feet of water and could carry heavy loads.

The immediate effects of this victory were stunning. The British virtually panicked, withdrawing all the garrisons on the Delaware before the American "farmers" could wipe them out. Cornwallis, due to leave for England, was sent to take over British troops in New Jersey. American recruiters, who a week before could scarcely find a man, were now practically trampled underfoot by companies of volunteers.

The lasting effect of this snowy engagement begun on December 26, 1776, is underscored by a sober toast given by Cornwallis to his captor, General Washington, at a victory banquet in a field tent at Yorktown five years later: "When the illustrious part which your excellency has borne in the long and arduous contest becomes a matter of history, fame will gather your brightest laurels from the banks of the Delaware rather than those of the Chesapeake."

The Valley Forge Encampment

*T*HE VERY words "Valley Forge" conjure up a legend—a legend of men in rags, huddled in snowdrifts and subsisting on roots and berries. The true facts of that incredible winter on the rolling plateau above the swift Schuylkill need no embroidery. The German, von Steuben, said that no army in Europe would have held together under the conditions of Valley Forge.

They left bivouac at Whitemarsh, a tattered, worn, and spent army of about eleven thousand, and spent a full week staggering through snow, sleet, and icy rain to cover the scant thirteen miles to Valley Forge. Fires were built on arrival and the first night was spent huddled around them. The site was well chosen strategically, being unapproachable on two sides by virtue of steep hillsides and the almost unpassable Schuylkill River. The other slopes, which could be fortified, covered access roads to British-held Philadelphia. While the ground had military advantages, the climate did not. Washington and most of his staff would have preferred wintering in Wilmington, Delaware, to the south. Only the fear of losing New Jersey and Pennsylvania support, and the need to keep close watch on the Philadelphia enemy garrison, dictated a stay at Valley Forge.

The men who threw themselves into the snow under the trees on the heavily wooded plateau desperately needed food, clothing, and shelter. By heroic efforts, most of the army were in huts within a month. An unlimited supply of firewood at hand enabled them to survive a vicious and early winter. Twelve men crowded each hut, sleeping fitfully on rude bunks of poles

General Washington's marquee, or tent, where he lived for several weeks until his men were all in hastily built huts.

or on a scanty mat of straw, the smoke swirling around the dark, windowless room, only partially escaping up the poorly designed chimney. Only when his men were in huts did Washington leave his canvas tent and move into a local stone house.

The quartermaster's department had utterly collapsed; barrels of clothing had been abandoned because of muddy roads impassable by wagon. Half of Washington's army was without breeches, shoes, and stockings, thousands more without blankets. Sentries stood guard duty in the snow in their bare feet, with ragged scarves tied around their heads. The food supply was no better; at Christmas the entire camp was reduced to a stock of fewer than twenty-five barrels of flour. Salted pork was virtually unobtainable, dried herring had rotted in the casks, and fresh meat was almost unknown. The local farms were already stripped bare and what livestock had been concealed

In the artillery park on the high ground of Valley Forge, General Henry Knox kept his cannon ready to defend any part of the camp threatened. These replicas are placed exactly where the originals stood in 1777-78.

Chief Surgeon Bodo Otto and his men of the medical department used every available structure for the care of the sick. This small schoolhouse, built in 1705, and situated in the heart of the four thousand-acre camp, was a hospital.

was usually driven to market in Philadelphia for British gold. The troops existed on fire-cake, patties of flour and water partially baked on hot stones around the fires. Even the water was in short supply, having to be hauled up the steep hill from the river below. "Camp fever" and the "putrid fever" ravaged the camp. These diseases were typhoid and typhus and, along with smallpox, they took a heavy toll. When the sick overcrowded the huts and a school-house hospital, they were sent down to Yellow Springs or to the Moravian Brethren at Bethlehem where dedicated patriots nursed them as best they could. Crowding in typhus victims with the wounded from Brandywine battlefield frequently resulted in death for all, nurses and doctors included. No one was aware of the dangers of contagion.

Through the early weeks of the new year of 1778, men died by the hundreds. Burial parties stripped the needed rags from the dead before laying them in shallow graves. All of the artillery horses died for want of forage. They were too many to bury in the frozen ground, and they presented still

*Valley Creek still winds by, a short distance
from the door of the John Potts house.*

Here, on the outer line of defense, were the huts of General Peter Muhlenberg's brigade.

another health hazard. In February, Washington declared the camp "in famine."

The efforts of several exceptional men, who could not acknowledge defeat, prevented the total disintegration of the army. Allen McClane lay in wait for the British raiding parties, letting them secure cattle, then taking their prizes from them. "Light-Horse Harry" Lee and Anthony Wayne became expert at cattle rustling. Nathanael Greene was appointed chief forager, and Jeremiah Wadsworth was made responsible for procuring clothing and foodstuffs. They worked near miracles and kept the army alive until the spring run of shad up the Schuylkill arrived.

Two other events served to keep the Continental army together during these harrowing months. The first was the arrival of a chunky, middle-aged German soldier of fortune named Steube. He had letters from Ben Franklin and others testifying that he was a lieutenant general, a nobleman, and owner of a Swabian estate who wished to aid Washington. The only precisely accu-

Washington himself is said to have designed the twelve-man huts erected at Valley Forge. Bunks were made with poles and split saplings. The walls were chinked with mud or clay, and windows were cut only when spring arrived.

rate part of his introduction was a genuine desire to help. General Washington recognized his military ability and accepted his offer to serve without rank or pay other than a subsistence. This ex-captain who called himself "von Steuben" was given the chance to prove himself, and he did. He trained the troops to one mode of drill, cured them of their often fatal habit of advancing in single file, and created a discipline that would last until victory. A grateful Congress took note of the incredible transformation von Steuben had wrought in the army and appointed him a major general.

The second significant event occurred in February, when France recog-

Partly underground to cut down on the drafts that blew through their loosely sealed walls, these huts offered inadequate protection from the elements.

Without blankets and only partially clothed in rags, continually hungry and chilled, the patriot soldiers suffered five bitter months in these huts.

nized the independence of the United States. They were no longer alone in their opposition to England.

Finally, in June, the British evacuated Philadelphia, and from the wooded plateau of Valley Forge, where three thousand patriot soldiers lay buried, a new Continental army came after them. Hardened in the campfires of the Forge, it struck savagely and fought the flower of the British forces to a draw, victory eluding their grasp only by the dereliction of an American general. After this, it was never again the British army against the rebels, but the British army opposed by the Continental Army of the United States.

Washington, leading his weary army into winter quarters. (Detail of an equestrian statue at Morristown, New Jersey)

Over nine hundred log cabins covered the slopes of Valley Forge during the winter encampment.

These authentic replicas have been constructed on the actual sites of original huts at Valley Forge.

Headquarters House at Valley Forge

A SMALL village on the west side of the Schuylkill River, about twenty miles from Philadelphia, became known forever when the weary men of the Continental army wintered nearby in 1777. A forge had been in existence there since 1742, but only later was it named after the creek running alongside. Valley Forge was owned by John Potts at the time of the encampment. He built a sawmill and a gristmill on the Valley Creek as well.

The Potts family turned over their sturdy stone house to Washington for his use, while other officers were quartered in the log huts or in the half-dozen stone houses on the plateau.

John Potts' house was offered to Washington for his headquarters while at Valley Forge. It was about twenty years old at that time.

Washington used John Potts' secretary desk in the front parlor. The cloak and sword hang at the side door entrance.

The kitchen of the Potts house. Here, meals were prepared and several of the officers' wives constantly produced knitted stockings and scarves for the soldiers.

*This is the kettle Martha Washington brought to the encampment and which
she used in brewing tea for her husband and his aides.*

Despite setbacks and adversity, Washington kept meticulous records of his military accounts. This rear room opposite the kitchen was his office and council room at Valley Forge.

The second-floor front bedroom was used by Martha Washington.

Washington slept in this second-floor bedroom of the Potts house. The officers of the Continental army lived in relative austerity compared to the King's imperial officer corps. The British frequently suffered military setbacks because of the huge baggage train that followed in their wake. When Clinton withdrew from Philadelphia, his army's baggage filled fifteen hundred wagons.

The Morristown Encampment

*T*HE CONTINENTAL army had sheltered in the Morristown hills of New Jersey in the winter of 1777 and now returned in 1779. The men would have preferred a milder climate to the south, but as long as the British controlled the New York region, the Continentals must remain in the area both to protect the citizenry and deny supplies to the enemy.

Since Valley Forge, the tide had seemingly turned for the rebels. Spain and France were at war with Britain, and Burgoyne had surrendered his troops at Saratoga. These improvements were offset by the utter collapse of the Continental treasury. Hard money was almost unobtainable and paper notes literally "not worth a Continental." A ratio of ten paper dollars to one silver soon soared to sixty, eighty, and one hundred to a dollar of hard currency. Even the paper notes were not forthcoming from Congress, and men went six months to a year without pay. Desertions rose and officers (who could resign their commissions at will) left because they could not pay for their food and clothing. Public dispatches were not sent for weeks because there was no money to pay the couriers.

With all these problems this encampment faced a new one; the worst winter storms in seventy-five years descended on the Jersey hills. A three-day blizzard struck in January before the troops had erected their log huts, and men were actually buried in their tents. The roads and split-rail fences were invisible under six feet of snow. The mercury dropped and stayed below freezing for weeks. The Passaic, Delaware, and the mighty Hudson River, all froze solid from bank to bank. Twenty-eight separate snowfalls occurred between December and April that terrible winter. The troops were as badly off for want of clothing, blankets, and food as at Valley Forge. Only the efforts of Jersey's population kept the army alive, donating what could be spared from their winter stores.

Despite the condition of the army, Washington knew the dangers of prolonged inaction. A major raid was launched against Staten Island, but the enemy was forewarned and the element of surprise essential to the operation was lost. Major General William Alexander returned with little to show other than a few prisoners.

The snows had barely gone when Lafayette returned in May, 1780, from a year in France. A second French army and fleet would be sent to aid the colonists. This good news was followed by word of a debacle in the South. General Lincoln and five thousand men had been captured by the British. The enemy in New York thought Washington's winter-weary troops could

The Jockey Hollow farmhouse of Henry Wick housed Major General Arthur St. Clair of the Pennsylvania line during the 1779 winter.

The Wick house was built in 1750 and was a typical prosperous farmer's home. These split-rail fences were buried in the heavy snows of 1779-80.

Dr. James Tilton designed this structure to serve as a hospital for the troops camped in Jockey Hollow. A fire burned in the center of the earth floor and the patients lay in a circle around it, feet toward the blaze. There being no chimney, the smoke swirled around the sick before leaving through louvers in the roof. It was thought that smoke was helpful in combating infection.

now be taken, and an attack into Jersey was launched by General Knyphausen. The American regulars, joined by local militia, made his advance so costly that the offensive was ended and the British retreated to Staten Island. On this note the Continental army packed and left the hills and hollows of Morristown.

The Ford Mansion

Morristown, New Jersey

THE FORD mansion in Morristown had only been completed a few years when it was pressed into use as Washington's headquarters. It had been built by a wealthy patriot, Colonel Jacob Ford, Jr. He was a prosperous manufacturer of powder and iron in his own works near Morristown. He died of illness contracted on active duty as commander of the Morris County militia, leaving his widow with four children.

Washington chose the town and hills of Morristown for several reasons. Nearby were the iron-working furnaces and forges needed by the army, as well as gristmills and sawmills. There was ample wood for building shelters and providing fuel. Not least was the almost total absence of Tory sentiment in the area. The Watchung Mountains between the camp and New York would forestall a surprise enemy attack and he could move north or south on a good road network when necessary.

While Washington settled in the Ford home with his wife Martha and his aides, several farms in an area known as Jockey Hollow were selected for the bivouac of the Continental troops. The general arrived in town during a vicious snow and hail storm, a foretaste of the winter to come. Huts were constructed opposite the Ford mansion for the "life guard" detachment.

Washington's chief problem this winter, besides feeding and clothing his men and keeping close watch on the enemy, was the endless struggle to keep an army intact. Many of the men were short-term enlistment militia. When their terms expired they were free to leave, and many did. The shortage of

Washington used this modest room as a headquarters to receive officers from the field and plan strategy during the winter of 1779-80.

The spacious living room of the Ford mansion. Washington wrote much of his correspondence at the secretary desk on the far wall.

money prevented increasing the enlistment bounty. Men who had carried the struggle for several years, the seasoned veterans, were going home to tend neglected farms and see their families. Washington sent his generals home to recruit and devoted himself to a flood of correspondence to Congress pleading for funds to rebuild his worn army.

The huge kitchen, where eighteen people of Washington's party and all of Widow Ford's circle of friends crowded together in an effort to stay warm during the cruel days of that hard winter.

The second-floor guest room where Lafayette stayed when he returned from France in May of 1780.

Servant's room in the Ford mansion.

Built in 1774, the Ford mansion is an outstanding example of colonial stone and frame construction.

1780

Touro Synagogue

Newport, Rhode Island

*T*HE CODE of Laws under which Rhode Island was governed proclaimed religious freedom. A Jewish sect found haven here from oppression encountered in Europe. This unusual house of worship was built about a century after they settled in Newport. It was dedicated in 1763, under the leadership of the Reverend Isaac Touro. This sect declined after the Revolution and their synagogue was closed for many years. It enjoyed revitalization in the late nineteenth century and has been in constant use since that time as an active house of worship.

At the time of the Revolution, Jews in the colonies numbered about two thousand. They had fled religious persecution in Spain, Portugal, and Germany to seek freedom in America. In the American colonies they enjoyed civil rights but not full enfranchisement. New York was the first state to grant the latter, in 1777, and New Hampshire the last, in 1877.

Haym Salomon was a Polish Jew who had come to America as a refugee. He was a successful banker and had amassed a fortune by the time the war broke out. He gave money to delegates to Congress who could not afford to serve without payment, and helped Robert Morris negotiate foreign loans that were vital to the Revolutionary cause. He poured most of his own wealth into the needs of the fledgling government, accepting paper notes as security. When he died suddenly at the age of forty-five after the war, he left a young wife with four children and only the furniture in their home. His fortune was in government notes worthless at that time. James Madison and many in

In a severe modification of colonial Georgian architecture, a plain brick exterior contrasts with an ornate interior.

Twelve Ionic columns support a gallery. From this balcony twelve Corinthian
columns support a domed ceiling. Five brass candelabra light the interior.

Looking down from the gallery at the bimah, the elevated platform where the cantor reads the Torah.

Congress considered him one of the truest friends America had at the hour of her birth.

Washington expressed the philosophy of the new nation when he delivered this message to the congregation at Touro Synagogue in 1790: "May the children of the stock of Abraham, who dwell in this land, continue to merit and enjoy the good will of the other inhabitants, while every one shall sit in safety under his own vine and fig-tree and there shall be none to make them afraid."

The entrance portico is supported by wooden Ionic columns.

The austere lines are an unusual treatment of the Georgian design popular in colonial times.

The Townsend House

Oyster Bay, New York

FEW ARMIES have had the benefit of an intelligence service as efficient as that set up by Washington in the earliest days of the war.

The part of the spy chain centered on occupied Long Island enabled Washington to keep track of major British troop and fleet movements around the New York hub of enemy activity. Its creation was precipitated by the untimely capture and execution of Captain Nathan Hale. This youthful and dedicated officer had volunteered, after an urgent appeal from Washington himself, to obtain information that would reveal where and how the British planned to strike at New York.

The spacious colonial house erected about 1738.

A low-ceilinged, second-floor bedroom at Raynham Hall.

After Hale's capture, it was realized that a system of several people working in concert would more likely be successful. Colonel Benjamin Tallmadge in Connecticut ran the new operation, reporting directly to General Washington. Skilled whaleboat sailors under Caleb Brewster brought the information across the Sound. Abraham Woodhull of Setauket collected Long Island intelligence from others. His principal agent, and possibly the most valuable spy Washington had, was Robert Townsend of Oyster Bay. While his family homestead at Oyster Bay was forced to billet British officers, this young man remained in New York throughout the war, tending his store and forwarding invaluable intelligence to Woodhull.

Code names were used, Robert Townsend being called Culper, Jr., and Abraham Woodhull, Culper, Sr. A patriot named Austin Roe was the usual messenger, and invisible ink and special codes were among the devices used to avoid detection. Loyalist patrols as well as British check posts made the work extremely dangerous.

How successful these men were in guarding their secrets is revealed by the astonishing fact that Samuel Townsend, father of Culper, Jr., is believed to have been totally ignorant of his son's patriotic activities.

The British officer who chose Raynham Hall, the Townsend house in Oyster Bay, for a billet was Lieutenant Colonel John Simcoe, commander of the Queen's Rangers. This elite troop, about five hundred strong, consisted of Loyalist volunteers and Irish and Scots regulars. Simcoe and his men

The curved settle was normally placed before the fire, its high back helping to confine the heat.

The dining room at the front of the house. The oak flooring was cut from trees on the property.

later earned a reputation during the war in the South as brilliant and ruthless foes. He was a correct guest, however, and the three Townsend daughters, Sally, Audrey, and Phoebe, held numerous tea parties for the colonel and his staff. Their father was a known patriot. He had been arrested once, and only the intervention of a Loyalist friend had kept him from a trip to the prison ships moored off Brooklyn. His family strove to be agreeable to the British while remaining devoted to the patriotic cause.

None of the officers were more charming to the girls than a friend and frequent guest of Simcoe, a Major John André. André was an aide to General Henry Clinton and highly regarded in British circles. During one visit

Seen here in reverse, as it would have appeared to Sally Townsend looking in the hall mirror, is the corner cupboard where Major André removed a secret message. This suspicious incident and details of an overheard conversation between Colonel Simcoe and André were transmitted to Robert Townsend by Sally.

The parlor room of Raynham Hall. The clock here was originally in the Peter Townsend home in upstate New York, where Washington is said to have set his watch by it on occasion.

The Townsend family doorknocker on the great Dutch door entrance.

to the Townsend house, André playfully hid a bowl of just fried Dutch doughnuts in a corner cupboard to tease young Sally. On another occasion he was observed by Sally removing a secret message from the same cabinet. This incident and other details overheard between Simcoe and André were transmitted by Sally to her brother, "Culper, Jr.," in New York. Added to other evidence, the Benedict Arnold plot to betray West Point was revealed and thwarted.

Major André paid with his life. He was executed as a spy by the Americans. Arnold, pretending to need intelligence around West Point, wrote Tallmadge for the names of his best spies. They were not forthcoming and the Long Island section of Washington's intelligence continued its daring work until the British evacuated New York in 1783.

After the war, members of this spy bureau that were known only to a few did not step forward and claim honor and glory. Major Tallmadge and others respected the oath and remained silent. Influential Tories, still strong in parts of the new nation, might well have attempted to injure these men.

Robert Townsend died in 1838 and never revealed to anyone his part in the eight-year war for freedom. A Long Island historian, Morton Pennypacker, is generally credited with proving the identity of Culper, Jr., when he established in 1930 that the correspondence of Robert Townsend and the spy letters to Washington were written by the same hand.

When visiting his friend, Colonel Simcoe, Major André used this room just
behind the parlor.

1780

Saddle Rock Grist Mill

Great Neck, New York

*T*WO CENTERS of colonial life were the forge and the gristmill. Fittings for windows and doors, wagons and weapons were made and repaired in the blacksmith's forge. Every agricultural community had its nearby gristmill. Located on a swift stream, it used water power to rotate the huge stones that turned grain into flour. A mill and a forge were vital for an army in encampment and the location of many Revolutionary bivouacs were chosen because of their proximity to one or the other.

This mill on the northern shore of Long Island is unusual in one major respect. Its motive power is running water, but it is tied to the rise and fall of the tides. When the tide rises in Long Island Sound, water enters and fills a pond. It is confined by a sluice gate until milling is to begin. When the gate is raised, the pent-up water rushes out through a narrow channel past the undershot water wheel, turning the wheel and the mill stone it is fixed to. The waters of the millpond are sufficient to grind grain for several hours. The canal was large enough to permit sloops to enter at high tide and deliver their grain at a side loading door.

While the conveyor belts and flour chutes date from the 1850's, this mill was in operation during the Revolution. John and David Allen ran it then and quite probably ground the grain of farmer and redcoat alike.

When the gate is raised, rushing waters of the tidal pond turn the gristmill water wheel.

At low tide the canal is empty and the mill is ready to operate from its tidal pond water supply.

These heavy balance scales weighed the farmers' grain until 1870.

*Flour chutes and wooden implements at the mill. The shovel was made from
a single plank.*

The Prison Ships of Wallabout Bay

*E*ARLY in the war, the British were faced with the problem of rebel prisoners captured on Long Island and the crews of colonial privateers taken at sea. Churches in New York and unseaworthy ships were converted to prisons, which rapidly became pesthouses of disease and suffering. In the course of the eight-year struggle, thousands of patriots were taken to these hulks and few came away alive.

Among the prison ships anchored in Wallabout Bay was a former 64-gun man-of-war, the *Jersey*. American soldiers, sailors, and citizens, even women, were packed in below decks, over twelve hundred at one time being aboard. Locked under gratings at night, clad only in the clothing they wore when captured, sick and well together, they struggled to survive. A meager diet of wormy bread, oatmeal, and poor bully beef cooked in sea water left them unable to resist the smallpox and yellow fever that periodically raged through their crowded quarters.

In British eyes, this disgraceful treatment of colonial prisoners was justified. Only in 1782 did they grant belligerent status and recognize the captured as prisoners of war. The fact that Washington had increasing numbers of British prisoners to exchange may have contributed to the new attitude.

When the few remaining inmates were liberated from the *Jersey*'s black hull in 1783, the vessel was abandoned. It lay off the banks of Wallabout Bay for several years, its rotted planks and timbers covered with thousands of

names carved by former inmates. Worms finally ate through her hull and she slipped to the bottom of the bay.

Freedom from British prisons was available to those who would embrace the Loyalist cause. Before accepting that price, over eleven thousand patriots died in the *Jersey* and other prison ships.

1781

Berkeley Plantation

James River, Virginia

WHILE the seaports of New England were growing and the merchants of Boston were building their tidy brick houses on winding streets, a radically different way of life was developing in the lush Virginia countryside along the banks of the James River. In New England it was trade and the skills of the sea that counted; in the southern colonies it was land and the tobacco leaf.

King James I awarded a grant in 1619 to the Berkeley Company. They set foot ashore at Harrison's Landing on December 4 in 1619, and declared the day would be annually and perpetually kept as a day of thanksgiving—more than a year before the Pilgrims dropped anchor off Plymouth Rock.

The great manor house of Berkeley, one of the oldest in Virginia, was built in 1726 by Benjamin Harrison. His son of the same name was a delegate to the Continental Congress, three times governor of Virginia, and a signer of the Declaration of Independence. (This Harrison's younger son, William Henry, became President of the United States. The grandson of William Henry, Benjamin Harrison, was also elected President.)

George Washington was a close friend of the second Benjamin Harrison and a frequent visitor at Berkeley. Problems of plantation management were often a topic of conversation. Washington's Mount Vernon, consisting of eight thousand acres, was a mere garden, compared to estates of the Tidewater country. Shirley Plantation, near Richmond, was exporting tobacco

Berkeley mansion is simple Georgian in style, with six dormers and unusually tall twin chimneys.

as early as 1616 and would eventually grow to a staggering 170,000 acres in size.

In 1780, Cornwallis belatedly realized that a storehouse of rebel wealth—the scores of tobacco warehouses along the rivers of Virginia—were virtually unprotected. He launched a series of major raids from New York under Brigadier General Benedict Arnold. The skills and daring that traitor had employed at Lake Champlain to serve liberty were turned against the patriots with devastating effect. Two British officers were detailed to advise Arnold, but he scarcely needed them. His troops were Tory volunteer units from New York and Pennsylvania, the crack British Light Infantry, and Simcoe's

The interior is more elegant than the exterior, with handsome woodwork installed by Benjamin Harrison the sixth.

This narrow door leads to a men's study. Its width was supposedly intended to keep the hoop-skirted ladies out.

The wide entrance hall at Berkeley was used for dancing on occasion.

Below the boxwood gardens the grounds drop to the banks of the James River. Here the remains of the dock pilings indicate where sloops were built during the Revolution.

Queen's Rangers. This last unit was commanded by Colonel Simcoe, who had quartered himself in the Townsend House at Oyster Bay on Long Island while Washington's chief spy operated an intelligence ring under his very nose.

Arnold's campaign with seasoned men against raw militia was brilliant. Cornwallis greatly increased his strength, and even Lafayette and von Steuben could not cope with the enemy. Enormous amounts of tobacco were burned, rifles and clothing captured. Berkeley was plundered, and several sloops under construction were destroyed. All this occurred at a time when confidence in the rebel cause had sunk to a point where the army could not buy a cavalry horse for 150,000 Continental paper dollars.

Cornwallis, despite the damage he did, was unable to destroy the force of about four thousand commanded by the shrewd and wily Lafayette. The British general chose to fortify nearby Yorktown and thus set the stage for the astonishing reversal of fortune to come within the year.

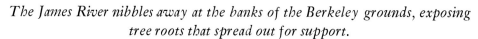

The James River nibbles away at the banks of the Berkeley grounds, exposing tree roots that spread out for support.

The Thomas Nelson, Jr., House

Yorktown, Virginia

*T*HOMAS Nelson, Jr., a Virginia-born aristocrat, was educated in England and returned to Virginia to become a member of the Council of the Province at the age of twenty-six.

Nelson came from a line of wealthy merchant planters with little to gain from espousing the rebel cause, yet he became a staunch friend of liberty. A close companion of Jefferson, he undoubtedly absorbed some of his ideas. He was a signer of the Declaration of Independence and governor of Virginia, succeeding Jefferson.

In 1781, Nelson organized the militia to combat the invasion of British armies from New York. When the fateful decision to defend Yorktown was made by Cornwallis, Nelson supported Washington's siege army with his three Virginia brigades, totaling three thousand men.

During the shelling of Yorktown, Nelson is said to have urged Washington to bombard his own home, because Cornwallis had made his headquarters in it. He spent both his health and his money on the patriot cause. When he died of asthma at sixty, only this brick house remained of his property and vast fortune. He left a wife and eleven children.

The Nelson home is typical of Tidewater mansions, resembling the Berkeley house on the James River.

The living room of the Nelson house has a concealed panel that gave access to a stairway between the walls.

Washington is shown firing the first round at the entrenched British positions at Yorktown. (From a diorama at Yorktown Battlefield Park)

1781
Yorktown Battlefield

*I*N MAY of 1781, a momentous conference was held in Wethersfield, Connecticut, by Washington and the French commander in America, General de Rochambeau. New French forces, including a fleet capable of meeting the Royal Navy on even terms and a French army, would make a combined sea and land operation possible for the first time.

A feint against New York caused British General Clinton to send for some of Cornwallis' army now in Virginia. In August, Washington heard that a French fleet under Count de Grasse would be in the Chesapeake shortly, but only for a brief time. Washington quickly realized that in Virginia, with control of the sea, he might finally corner and smash the enemy. He began a carefully disguised movement of his troops, finally marching or sailing over eight thousand men to the southern area, leaving about four thousand in the environs of New York to contain Clinton.

Meanwhile, the British navy had made a succession of errors in seeking the French fleet, known to be coming. As a result, French Admiral de Grasse made a safe arrival in Chesapeake Bay. When a fleet under Admiral Graves finally arrived, a prolonged battle took place. Both sides sustained moderate damage, but the British flagship, the *London,* was so mauled that Graves decided to break off the engagement and withdraw his fleet to New York.

This surprising decision meant that the French could seal off Yorktown from the sea. Cornwallis, with limited ammunition, dwindling food stores, and a lack of medicine, could not hope to be supplied or evacuated by sea.

*Small seige howitzers in position at Yorktown. Massed artillery played a de-
cisive role in the victory at Yorktown.*

He was on his own, with ten thousand seasoned veterans. Losses at the battle of Guilford Courthouse, however, had badly depleted his staff of experienced officers.

As the strength of the Americans grew daily, Lafayette adding his three thousand troops and Thomas Nelson bringing in three thousand Virginia militia, Cornwallis prepared a classic defense in depth. He was not yet seriously concerned for his safety, as he was receiving letters from Clinton in New York assuring him of relief. On September 29, Cornwallis withdrew into his main works without defending his outer line. The next two weeks saw a massive and skillful attack mounted by the allied armies. Cornwallis fought a gallant defense but, realizing help was not coming, he attempted a night escape across the river to Gloucester Point. Insufficient boats and a severe storm disrupted this effort. On the following morning he sent officers under a flag of truce to discuss terms of surrender. A rescue fleet of twenty-five capital ships and an army of seven thousand sailed from New York on the very day of the surrender, just one week too late.

A British gun position at Yorktown.

Fraunces Tavern

New York City, New York

THIS is one of the oldest buildings standing on Manhattan Island and the scene of one of the most emotion-packed meetings of the Revolution. On his way home after victory, Washington met his officers here and bade them farewell.

It was no elaborate ceremony and he made no long address. According to witnesses, Washington was so choked with emotion that he had difficulty delivering any address. Each of the forty-four ranking officers was then invited to take Washington's hand in turn. Most had been through the entire war with him, from the earliest dark days of defeat and privation. Anthony Wayne, Knox of the artillery, von Steuben and Kosciuszko, Gates, Lincoln, and Putnam were all here. They feared they would never see him again and some never did. The silent and tearful scene in the long room of the tavern was finally concluded. Washington left, passing through files of soldiers, and a still silent crowd of officers and citizens followed him to Whitehall ferry where he boarded his barge. When out in the stream, he waved farewell. New York would see him return in six years to take the oath of office as the nation's first President.

The tavern in which he parted from his officers began life as a private mansion, built by Stephen de Lancey, a French Huguenot who had married into the Van Cortlandt family. This was in 1719. The house was occupied successively by his son and then his brothers and sisters. It was used briefly as a warehouse before Samuel Fraunces purchased it for 2,000 pounds in

One of Manhattan's oldest surviving buildings, this tavern was the scene of Washington's farewell to his officers in December, 1783.

1762. Several incidents of note occurred at the tavern before the Revolution. In 1774, the Sons of Liberty met there and planned a little known tea party, which saw the cargo of the ship *London* dumped in New York harbor.

During the seven years of British occupation, Fraunces continued to run his inn, then named the Queen's Head Tavern. After peace was restored and the Revolutionary leaders were his guests once more, Fraunces appealed to Washington for a "Certificate and Recommendation" to end the calumny he was subject to. Washington did give him a warm letter and expressed his high regard for Samuel Fraunces by making him steward of his household when he became President.

Known as "Old Ironsides," the frigate Constitution, *designed by Joshua Humphreys of Philadelphia, was built to outfight and outsail any European vessel of the day.*

"*Old Ironsides*"

Boston, Massachusetts

THE FRIGATE *Constitution* was built after the Revolution and was a symbol of the sovereignty of the new nation. After victory, the country reduced its army to a handful of troops and disposed of its fledgling navy entirely. Convinced they would conduct themselves so as to make no enemies, the Americans assumed they had no need for a standing army or navy. But without the power to insist on the right of free passage on the sea, the Algerian pirates raided their merchant ships without mercy.

In 1794, President Washington asked Congress to provide protection for American ships and assure freedom of the seas by building a fleet of six men-of-war. They were to have great firepower, as well as the ability to run

Part of the gun deck where thirty 24-pounders were served. Over four hundred seamen swung their hammocks on this deck.

Block and tackle controlled heavy guns during firing and recoil.

from any combination of more powerful ships. They contributed mightily to defeating the Barbary pirates and insuring respect for the American flag on the high seas.

When the War of 1812 broke out, the odds against a victory at sea appeared overwhelming. Britain had about 750 effective warships, America less than twenty. The *Constitution* won her name of "Old Ironsides" in a victorious battle with the *Guerriere* when an American sailor saw shot bounce off the heavy oak sides of his ship and exclaimed that she was made of iron.

When a ship born of the white oak forests of Maine, designed, built, and manned by native Americans, could best the Royal Navy with its history of a thousand victories, the United States became not only a new nation but a new power in the eyes of the world.

A detail from a painting in the Philadelphia Maritime Museum shows the
Guerriere *surrendering to the* Constitution *during the War of 1812.*

The captain's quarters in the stern of the Constitution.

Typical officer's cabin below decks.

Two stern chasers covered the stern approach to "Old Ironsides."

Where to Find These Landmarks

Battle of Trenton—Route 546 on Delaware River south of Titusville, Mercer County, New Jersey

Berkeley Plantation—On State Route 5 between Richmond and Williamsburg, Virginia

Buckman's Tavern—Hancock Street, Lexington Green, Lexington, Massachusetts

Carpenters' Hall—Chestnut and Fourth Streets, Philadelphia, Pennsylvania

Christ Church—Market Street at Second Street, Philadelphia, Pennsylvania

Concord Bridge and Battle Road—Area along Lexington Road between Concord and Arlington, Massachusetts

Conference House—At end of Hylan Boulevard, Tottenville, Staten Island, New York

Elfreth's Alley—Between Front and Second Streets, north of Arch Street, Philadelphia, Pennsylvania

Faneuil Hall—Dock Square, Boston, Massachusetts

Ford Mansion—Morris Street, Morristown, New Jersey

Fraunces Tavern—54 Pearl Street, New York City, New York

George Wythe House—Palace Green, Colonial Williamsburg, Virginia

Gunboat *Philadelphia*—Smithsonian Institution, Washington, D.C.

Hancock-Clarke House—35 Hancock Street, Lexington, Massachusetts

Headquarters House—Valley Forge Interchange of Pennsylvania Turnpike to Port Kennedy, Montgomery, and Chester Counties, Valley Forge, Pennsylvania

Independence Hall—420 Chestnut Street, Philadelphia, Pennsylvania

John Bartram House—54th Street and Eastwick Avenue, Philadelphia, Pennsylvania

John Dickinson House—East of Route 113 on Kitts Hummock Road, five miles southeast of Dover, Delaware

Lexington Green—Area surrounding the Common, Lexington, Massachusetts

Morristown Encampment—Jockey Hollow Road at Morristown, Morris County, New Jersey

"Old Ironsides"—United States Naval Shipyard, Boston, Massachusetts

Old North Church—193 Salem Street, Boston, Massachusetts

Old South Meeting-House—Milk and Washington Streets, Boston, Massachusetts

Old State House—Washington and State Streets, Boston, Massachusetts

Paul Revere House—19 North Square, Boston, Massachusetts

Prison Ships of Wallabout Bay—No remains of the prison ships exist

Saddle Rock Grist Mill—Gristmill Lane, Saddle Rock (two miles north of Great Neck on Bayview Avenue), Long Island, New York

St. John's Church—East Broad and 24th Streets, Richmond, Virginia

Thomas Nelson, Jr., House—Main and Nelson Streets, Yorktown, Virginia

Thompson-Neely House—Bowman's Hill, four miles north of Washington Crossing, Bucks County, Pennsylvania

Touro Synagogue—85 Touro Street, Newport, Rhode Island

Townsend House—West Main Street, Oyster Bay, Long Island, New York

Valley Forge Encampment—Valley Forge Interchange of Pennsylvania Turnpike to Port Kennedy, Montgomery, and Chester Counties, Valley Forge, Pennsylvania

Yorktown Battlefield—On Colonial Parkway from Williamsburg or on Route 17 from points north, Yorktown, Virginia

A Selected Bibliography for Additional Reading

Andrews, Wayne, and Cochran, Thomas C. *Concise Dictionary of American History*. New York: Charles Scribner's Sons, 1962.

Dorson, Richard M. ed. *America Rebels*. Greenwich, Connecticut: Fawcett Publications, Inc., 1966.

Forbes, Esther. *Paul Revere and the World He Lived In*. Boston: Houghton Mifflin Company, 1942.

Kaplan, M.; Malone, D.; and Milhollen, H. *The Story of the Declaration of Independence*. New York: Oxford University Press, 1954.

Ketchum, Richard M. *The American Heritage Book of Great Historic Places*. New York: The American Heritage Publishing Co., Simon and Schuster, 1965.

Pennypacker, Morton. *General Washington's Spies on Long Island and in New York*. Brooklyn, New York: Long Island Historical Society, 1939.

Sarles, Frank B., and Shedd, Charles E. *Colonials and Patriots*. Washington, D.C.: National Park Service, 1964.

Tourtellot, Arthur B. *Lexington and Concord*. New York: W. W. Norton & Co., Inc., 1963.

Ward, Christopher. *The War of the Revolution*. New York: The Macmillan Company, 1952.

Index